Australian Curriculum

A student workbook

Leanne Bondin & Adam Kealley

First published in 2023, reprinted in 2024

Insight Publications Pty Ltd
3/350 Charman Road
Cheltenham Victoria 3192
Australia

Tel: +61 3 8571 4950
Email: books@insightpublications.com.au

www.insightpublications.com.au

A catalogue record for this book is available from the National Library of Australia

Australian Curriculum English Year 8 / Leanne Bondin and Adam Kealley

ISBN: 9781922771698

Edited by Lisa Neale

Cover by Melisa Paredes

Internal design by Melisa Paredes

Typesetting by Kobie van Jaarsveld

Printed by Markono Print Media Pte Ltd

Contents

Note to teachers **iv**

Unit 1: Engaging the reader 1

Unit 2: Inspiring change 14

Unit 3: Fascinating photography 25

Unit 4: Making connections 36

Unit 5: Personal writing 46

Unit 6: The dystopian genre – frightening futures 57

Unit 7: Performance poetry 68

Unit 8: Australian film study 83

Unit 9: Dive into drama 96

Unit 10: Communicating clearly 111

Unit 11: Using comprehension strategies 120

Unit 12: Improving your writing 138

Glossary **154**

Acknowledgements **156**

Note to teachers

The Australian Curriculum English series is designed to assist student development of English skills, knowledge and understandings in interesting, engaging ways. The series aligns with Version 9.0 of the Australian Curriculum, ensuring that the Literature, Language and Literacy strands of the curriculum, as well as their sub-strands and threads, are seamlessly integrated and well balanced across the units of work. Each text in the series covers the entire curriculum content for its corresponding year level at least once, and in most instances several times, in order to highlight the varied approaches available to teachers and their students. Relevant Australian Curriculum content is specified in the introduction to each unit.

Each Australian Curriculum English book comprises 12 units, each of which is centred on a unifying theme, text type or significant English skill. Cumulatively, the units provide ample opportunity for students to practise their writing, reading, listening, speaking and viewing skills. The units can be completed in any order; teachers may find it useful to dip in and out of units in ways that complement their established teaching and learning programs.

The units include a number of text extracts, from familiar 'classics' to more contemporary and original texts. The extracts have been selected for their potential to illustrate particular curriculum content in action; teachers are encouraged to examine the texts independently to assess their suitability for their specific school context or cohort. While each unit includes multiple activities related to the unit focus, the final two units in the book closely target the specific comprehension strategies and grammar, punctuation and word knowledge specified in the Australian Curriculum English 7–10.

A range of colour-coded '**Check for understanding**' and '**Reflecting and discussing**' activities are embedded within the content of units 1–10. These activities are designed to:

» help students strengthen and deepen their understanding of the concepts covered

» encourage students to reflect carefully upon the content in relation to their own lives and experiences

» facilitate meaningful whole-class or small-group interactions and discussion around the content.

Several '**Get creative**' activities within units 1–10 prompt students to create their own texts in a range of forms by practising writing, speaking and creating for different audiences and purposes. All activities make ideal classroom and/or homework tasks. Many of the written activities included can be completed within the fill-in lines provided.

As English teachers ourselves, we appreciate the importance of practical and helpful resources that supplement our own classroom practices and assist students to master essential curriculum content and skills. We sincerely hope that this series does just that for you and your students. To access suggested solutions to the activities in this workbook, please email us at: sales@insightpublications.com.au

Engaging the reader

Engaging stories are the ones that we really don't want to put down – the ones that interest or immerse us in their worlds. This unit explains how fiction authors engage readers, just like you, through a range of language features, literary devices and text structures. The unit will also help you to recognise how texts reflect contexts that can be very different from our own. The 2002 novel *Parvana*, by Deborah Ellis, will be used as a case study to explore these points.

In this unit you will learn:

- how authors engage readers through language features, literary devices and text structures
- to recognise the values of individuals and groups in texts
- the way in which texts reflect historical, social and cultural contexts.

Curriculum content

Australian Curriculum content description	Content code
Share opinions about the language features, literary devices and text structures that contribute to the styles of literary texts.	AC9E8LE02
Analyse how language features such as sentence patterns create tone, and literary devices such as imagery create meaning and effect.	AC9E8LE05
Identify how texts reflect contexts.	AC9E8LY01
Analyse how authors organise ideas to develop and shape meaning.	AC9E8LY04

Engaging openings

To 'engage' a reader means to involve and interest them. This can be achieved through the crafting of an interesting opening, often called the 'exposition' or the 'orientation'. There are many ways in which a fiction text can offer an interesting opening that engages readers, making them want to keep reading. Here are some:

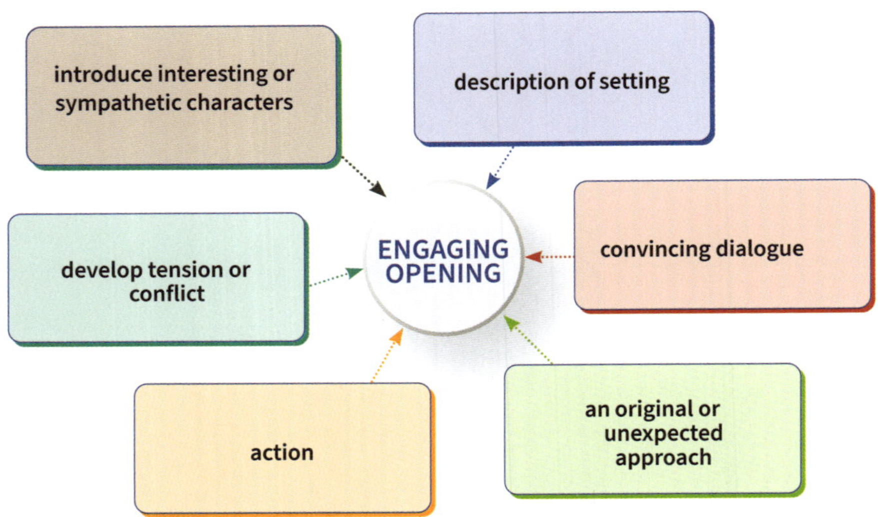

1.1 Check for understanding

1 Use a dictionary or thesaurus to find definitions and synonyms for the word 'engaging' and record them here.

______

______

______

2 Circle the aspects of a story below that are usually 'exposed' to us in its exposition.

climax　　setting　　characters

resolution　　conflict

3 Why might the opening of a **narrative** sometimes be called its 'orientation'?

______

______

The opening of *Parvana*

Novels are long pieces of writing, so they need to be engaging right from the start so that readers will become absorbed in the story and want to keep reading. Read the following example of an engaging opening from the novel *Parvana* by Deborah Ellis.

narrative The selection and sequencing of events or experiences, real or imagined, to tell a story to entertain, engage, inform and extend imagination, typically using an orientation, complication and resolution

'I can read that letter as well as Father can,' *Parvana* whispered into the folds of her chador. 'Well, almost.'

She didn't dare say those words out loud. The man sitting beside her father would not want to hear her voice. Nor would anyone else in the Kabul market. *Parvana* was there only to help her father walk to the market and back home again after work. She sat well back on the blanket, her head and most of her face covered by her chador.

She wasn't really supposed to be outside at all. The Taliban had ordered all the girls and women in Afghanistan to stay inside their homes. They even forbade girls to go to school. *Parvana* had had to leave her sixth-grade class, and her sister Nooria was not allowed to go to her high school. Their mother had been kicked out of her job as a writer for a Kabul radio station.

For more than a year now, they had all been stuck inside one room, along with five-year-old Maryam and two-year-old Ali.

Parvana did get out for a few hours most days to help her father walk. She was always glad to go outside, even though it meant sitting for hours on a blanket spread over the hard ground of the marketplace. At least it was something to do. She had even got used to holding her tongue and hiding her face.

She was small for her eleven years. As a small girl, she could usually get away with being outside without being questioned. 'I need this girl to help me walk,' her father would tell any Talib who asked, pointing to his leg. He had lost the lower part of his leg when the high school he was teaching in was bombed. His insides had been hurt somehow, too. He was often tired.

1.2 Check for understanding

1 Re-read the first line of the extract above. In which of the following ways has the author chosen to open the novel? Circle them

by introducing an interesting character

with dialogue

with a description of the weather

2 Fill in the names of the country and the city in which this extract is set.

a country: A ____________________.

b city: K ____________________.

3 Why might *Parvana* be proud of the fact that she can read the letter as well as her father can?

____

____

4 What makes the central character, *Parvana*, seem interesting in this opening?

____

____

5 Values are the principles and ideals that are considered important to individuals or groups. Circle the value/s you think might be important to *Parvana*, based on this extract:

friendship   freedom   education   independence

6 How is a sense of tension and danger created in the extract? Consider *Parvana*'s actions.

____

____

7 Which of the **values** listed above is the most important to you? Provide reasons for your choice.

____

____

Other approaches to opening a fiction text

values Ideas and beliefs specific to individuals and groups

An important feature of *Parvana*'s dialogue at the beginning of this novel is that it is not actually spoken to anyone. This technique is called 'internal dialogue'. It engages the reader's interest by making us wonder why she does not speak aloud; and we soon learn that *Parvana* has to keep her thoughts and feelings to herself so that she can survive.

Here are some examples of other interesting ways to begin a story.

» action – begins with a high-energy, gripping event:

It was the day my grandmother exploded.

The Crow Road, Iain Banks

» description of setting – sets the scene with a detailed description of place:

In a hole in the ground there lived a hobbit. Not a nasty, dirty, wet hole, filled with the ends of worms and an oozy smell, nor yet a dry, bare, sandy hole with nothing in it to sit down on or to eat: it was a hobbit-hole, and that means comfort.

The Hobbit, JRR Tolkien

» an unexpected or original approach – surprises readers by doing something unusual:

If you were interested in stories with happy endings, you would be better off reading some other book.

The Bad Beginning (A Series of Unfortunate Events), Lemony Snicket

1.3 Reflecting and discussing

Discuss the following questions in pairs, in small groups or with the whole class as directed by your teacher.

1. Which one of the three novel openings in the examples engages you the most, and why?
2. What other novels have you read or studied that use these approaches to engage their readers?
3. Which of these three approaches do you think you would most like to use to open your own fictional narrative? Give reasons for your answer.

1.4 Check for understanding

1. Read the following pairs of sentences. In each pair, tick the sentence that provides a more interesting beginning.

   a. It was time to get up and go to school. ☐
   'Get up! You can't be late today of all days,' Dad called from the kitchen. ☐

   b. The bushfire was roaring like a freight train across the country, throwing fireballs into the black smoke, the wind devouring everything in its path. ☐
   Once upon a time there was a blazing fire. ☐

   c. I was born five minutes after my mother got to the hospital. ☐
   Mum says I was always obedient; I even had the manners to wait until she got to hospital before I was born – it was only five minutes later, but still … ☐

1.5 Get creative

1 Read the following sentences. Replace each one with a new, more engaging introductory sentence. Use dialogue, action, description of setting or an unexpected, original approach for each sentence.

a I almost fell off the edge.

____

____

b Her mobile phone was gone.

____

____

c How would he explain the crash to his parents?

____

____

d It was the grand final.

____

____

e The message appeared again.

____

____

2 Choose one of your opening sentences above to continue developing. In your English notebook, draft the opening of a short story using your chosen opening sentence.

Language features

Language features are those features that support meaning in a text, such as vocabulary, figurative language and punctuation. Vocabulary, in particular, plays an important role in *Parvana* because the Dari words help us recognise the context reflected in the novel.

language features Features that support meaning (e.g. clause- and word-level grammar, vocabulary, figurative language, punctuation, images). Choices vary for the purpose, subject matter, audience and mode or medium

Re-read the extract from *Parvana*. You might not have seen words like 'chador' and 'Talib' before, but clues about what the words mean are contained in the extract. Someone reading *Parvana* might interpret the word 'chador' in the following way:

» example from the text extract: 'her head and most of her face covered by her chador'

» reader's interpretation: 'A chador is something that can cover a head and face, maybe like a hat or veil or piece of clothing.'

purpose An intended or assumed reason for a type of text
subject matter The topic or theme under consideration
audience An intended or assumed group of readers, listeners or viewers that a writer, designer, filmmaker or speaker is addressing

1.6

Check for understanding

1 Suggest what the following underlined terms could mean, based on the clues in the sentences.

a The area is stunning in spring, when the hills are speckled with blossom, or in autumn, when the vines and ruje turn crimson.

____

b The melody performed by the angklung ensemble was rattling and resonant.

____

2 The choice of language features in a text will depend on its purpose, subject matter and audience. Draw lines to identify the purpose, subject matter and audience of the *Parvana* extract.

purpose	life in Afghanistan
subject matter	young adult Western readers
audience	to engage, entertain and educate

Understanding how texts reflect different contexts

Context is the environment in which a text is composed or read. It includes the social, cultural or historical circumstances that shape a text at the time in which it is composed or the time in which it is being read or viewed. The main factors that make up social, cultural and historical contexts are listed in the diagram below.

context An environment or situation (social, cultural or historical) in which a text is responded to or created. Or wording surrounding an unfamiliar word, which a reader or listener uses to understand its meaning

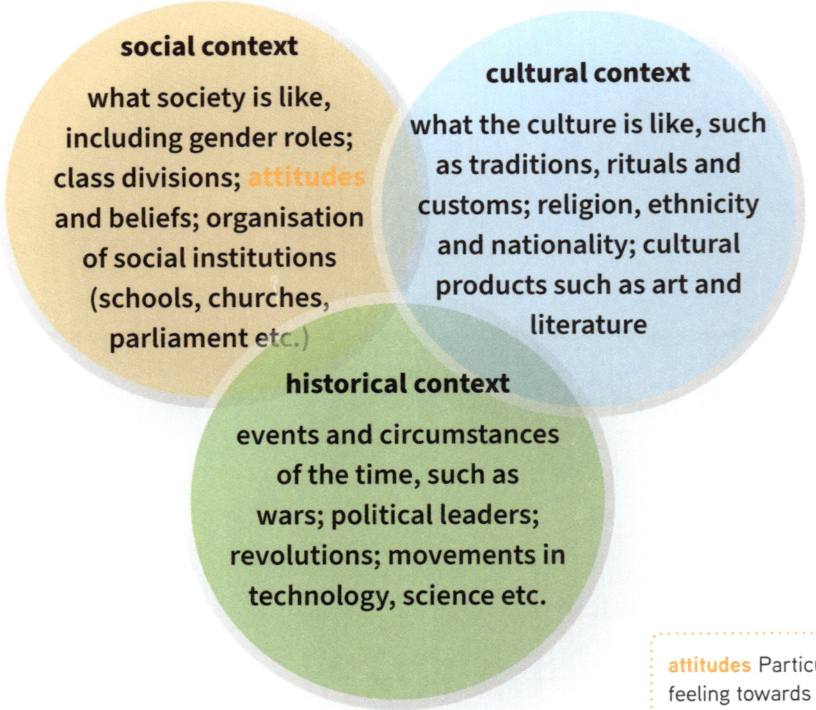

social context

what society is like, including gender roles; class divisions; attitudes and beliefs; organisation of social institutions (schools, churches, parliament etc.)

cultural context

what the culture is like, such as traditions, rituals and customs; religion, ethnicity and nationality; cultural products such as art and literature

historical context

events and circumstances of the time, such as wars; political leaders; revolutions; movements in technology, science etc.

The different types of context can be difficult to separate because they influence each other. The overlap between the circles in the diagram indicates the overlap between the contexts.

attitudes Particular ways of thinking and feeling towards people or things

Parvana probably reflects a very different context from your own. This is because *Parvana* was written over two decades ago by Canadian author Deborah Ellis, who visited Pakistan in 1997 to interview Afghan women in refugee camps. The novel reflects what was happening in the Afghan context during the rule of the Taliban in the late 1990s. Contextual factors are reflected in *Parvana* through its setting, characters, plot and **themes**.

theme The main idea, concept or message of a text

1.7 Check for understanding

Compare the context reflected in the novel with your own context by answering the guiding questions below.

Parvana's context	Your context
What was happening when the text was written? What big events were occurring? What was considered acceptable/unacceptable in society? Which of these aspects of context are reflected in the text through its setting, characters, plot and themes?	What is happening around you now? What big events are occurring? What is considered acceptable/unacceptable in society? Which of these influence your understanding of setting, characters, plot and themes in a text like *Parvana*?

2001 International Coalition war with Afghanistan after 9/11 attacks; international focus on al-Qaeda, whose home base is Afghanistan; global interest in gender inequality and male-dominated Afghan society – females not allowed to work, leave the house or go to school; Taliban control of Afghanistan; Sharia law which promotes patriarchal and ultra-conservative religious values.	

Imagery

Imagery is a very important literary device that is used to produce important effects in texts. It can create a particular atmosphere or type of character or tell us something about a setting, such as what it looks or sounds like. Imagery relates to our five senses. The main types of imagery are listed in the table below.

imagery Visually descriptive or figurative language to represent things including objects, actions and ideas in ways that appeal to the senses of the reader or viewer

Type of Imagery	Realted sense	Descriptions of:
visual imagery	sight	colours, size, appearance, physical features, landscapes
tactile imagery	touch	the physical feel of things, textures, roughness, smoothness
olfactory imagery	smell	aromas, scents, odours
gustatory imagery	taste	flavours, tastes, sweetness, sourness
auditory imagery	sound	noises, music, volume

The atmosphere created by sensory imagery can be so engaging that we feel like we become part of the story's world when reading. For example:

» Sensory descriptions of cars honking, lights flashing and crowds of people moving and talking within a big city could create a busy, bustling, atmosphere that makes readers feel overwhelmed.

- Sensory descriptions of the sounds of a waterfall, birds chirping and a light breeze touching a character's skin might create a peaceful, calm atmosphere that makes readers feel relaxed.
- Sensory descriptions of the delicious smells and warmth inside a bakery might create an inviting, comforting atmosphere that makes readers drool with hunger!

adjective A word class that describes, identifies or quantifies a noun or a pronoun, e.g. two (number or quantity), my (possessive), ancient (descriptive), shorter (comparative), wooden (classifying)

1.8 Get creative

1 Select one of the following topics or settings.

your first day of high school   a fairground

a shopping centre   the beach   a cinema

2 Write down three **adjectives** that describe the atmosphere of the topic or setting.

________________ ________________ ________________

3 Create a sentence about your chosen topic or setting for each of the following senses. Each sentence should contain imagery that helps describe the topic or setting in a way that engages the reader and creates an atmosphere.

a visual imagery: ________________________________

b tactile imagery: ________________________________

c olfactory imagery: ________________________________

d gustatory imagery: ________________________________

e auditory imagery: ________________________________

Narrative structure

Stories also engage us through another literary feature: their narrative structure. Narrative structure is the ordering or sequence of events in a story. The 'three-act structure' of a story, comprising a beginning, a middle and an end, goes back to Ancient Greek plays. It's the most basic and well-known structure for short stories, novels and film scripts, and our brains are wired to appreciate and feel engaged by stories that follow this structure.

Gustav Freytag, a German novelist, developed Freytag's Pyramid, a visual representation of this three-act structure. The 'beginning, middle and end' structure is sometimes also called the 'orientation, conflict and resolution' or the 'exposition, climax and denouement'. They all refer to the same basic structure.

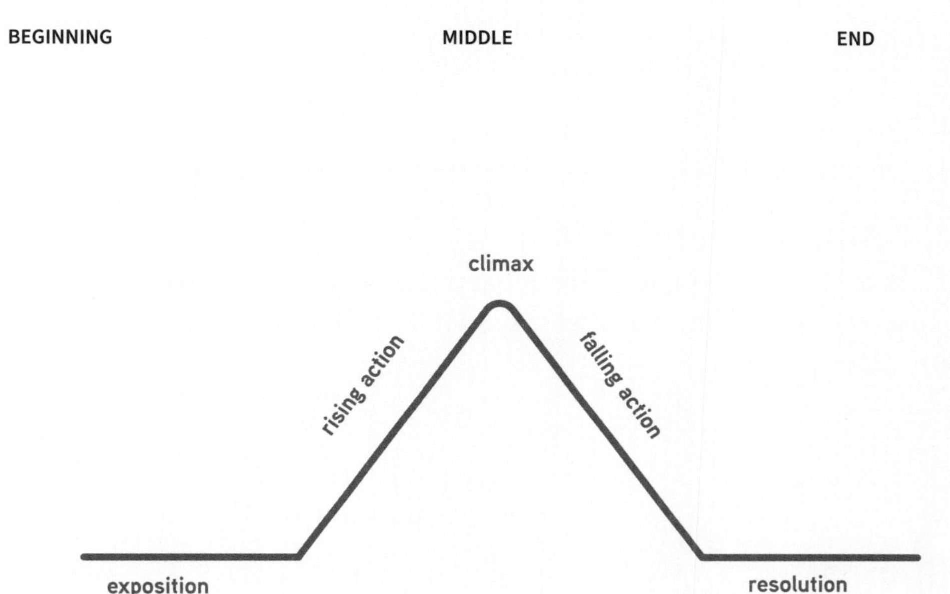

The beginning of the story sets up the exposition (introduction) to the characters and setting. The rising action builds towards a crisis or climax.

The middle of the story details the crisis or climax, the moment of greatest dramatic tension. The crisis or climax is the turning point in the story.

The falling action shows the consequences of this middle turning point and ties the story up in the resolution at the end.

Plot

Plot refers to the series of events that make up a story. Depending on how long a story is, there may be a number of plot points in each section of the three-act structure. Consider the narrative structure and plot of the Disney film *The Lion King*, as illustrated in the following diagram.

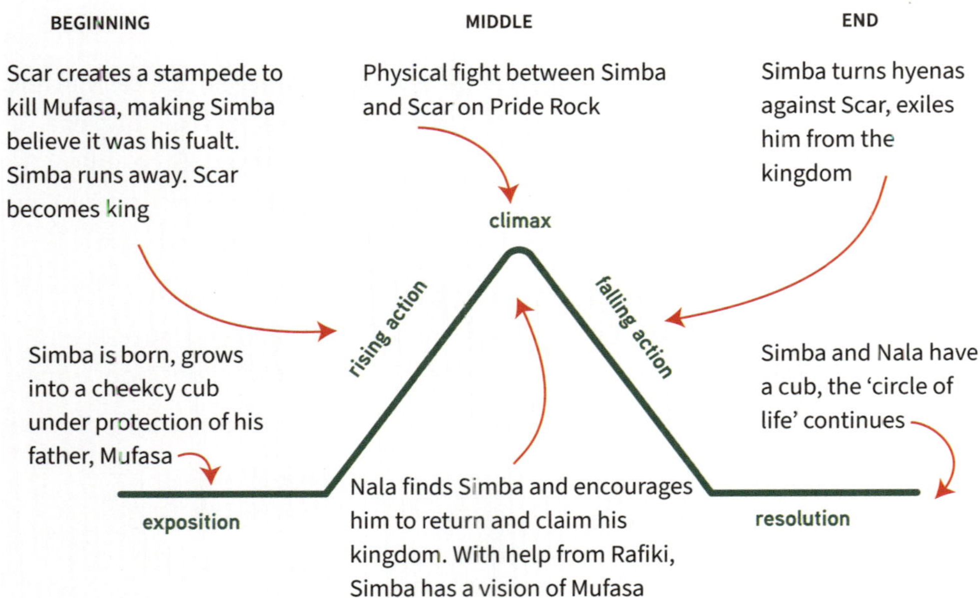

1.9 Check for understanding

1 Think of a short story, film or novel that you know well, and mark its major plot points on Freytag's Pyramid to see whether it follows the classic three-act structure.

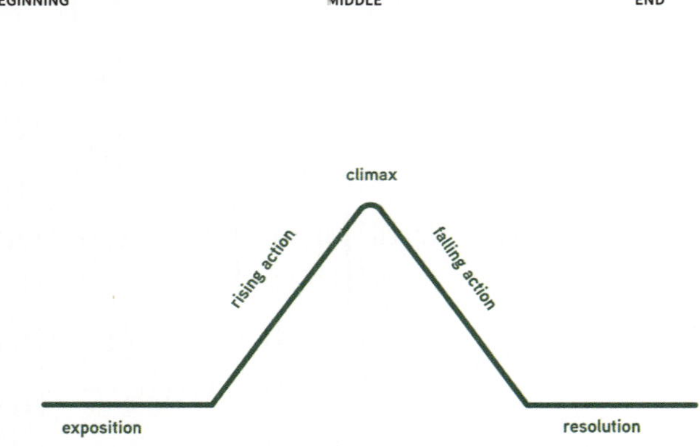

2 Some writers experiment with this structure to create certain effects, like surprise or curiosity or shock. Think about serial novels or television shows – do they always give you a satisfying ending or do they sometimes leave you hanging and wanting more? Give an example of a television show, novel or film with this sort of engaging ending.

___

1.10 Reflecting and discussing

Discuss the following questions in pairs, in small groups or with the whole class as directed by your teacher.

1 Re-read the extract, (page 3) and share your opinion about whether *Parvana* is presented as a sympathetic protagonist. Give reasons for your opinion.

2 Think about your favourite novel or film. Is the main character sympathetic or not? Provide reasons for your answer.

3 Do you think an antagonist can be a sympathetic character? Give reasons for your answer.

Engaging endings

A clever way to end a story is to introduce a 'twist', which has the effect of surprising or shocking the reader. The twist might involve the following approaches.

- reversal of identity – someone who turns out to be someone else (a relative, an old friend) or something else (a ghost, an animal, a figment of the imagination)
- reversal of motive – we thought someone wanted one thing but that was a deception and they really wanted something else
- reversal of perception – the story is actually taking place in a time or location that we did not expect.

1.11 Check for understanding

1 List three novels or films that have twists at the end and describe what sort of twist each one has. (These twists may be different from the three 'reversals' listed earlier.)

____

____

____

2 'I woke up and it was all a dream' is a clichéd twist ending. Why do you think this ending isn't satisfying for readers?

____

____

UNIT 2

Inspiring change

Who or what inspires you? Maybe it's a person who has overcome a lot of challenges or a public figure who has worked hard to become an expert in a skill or sport. Perhaps a powerful song or speech has inspired you. We are surrounded by texts and people that inspire us. Often, they make us want to change ourselves or our circumstances for the better. This unit will help you to revise persuasive techniques and to notice how they are used in inspirational speeches, songs and images.

In this unit you will learn:

- about persuasive devices used to inspire change
- to recognise the effects of nominalisation
- how to explore the meanings and effects of various inspirational texts.

Curriculum content

Australian Curriculum content description	Content code
Understand the effect of nominalisation in texts.	AC9E8LA06
Explain the ways that ideas and points of view may represent the values of individuals and groups in literary texts, drawn from historical, social and cultural contexts, by First Nations Australian, and wide-ranging Australian and world authors.	AC9E8LE01
Analyse and evaluate the ways that language features vary according to the purpose and audience of the text, and the ways that sources and quotations are used in a text.	AC9E8LY03

What does it mean to 'inspire' change?

The word 'inspire' has a lot of **synonyms**, including:

synonym A word having nearly the same meaning as others (e.g. synonyms for 'old' include 'aged', 'venerable', 'antiquated')

2.1 Reflecting and discussing

Discuss the following questions in pairs, in small groups or with the whole class as directed by your teacher.

1 Who or what inspires you? Give reasons for your answer

2 Below is a list of public figures who are considered inspirational. Share your thoughts about what you think makes one or more of these people an inspiration to others. (You may need to undertake some research to answer this question.)

Turia Pitt   Ghandi   Eddie Mabo

Mother Teresa   Cathy Freeman

Inspiring change

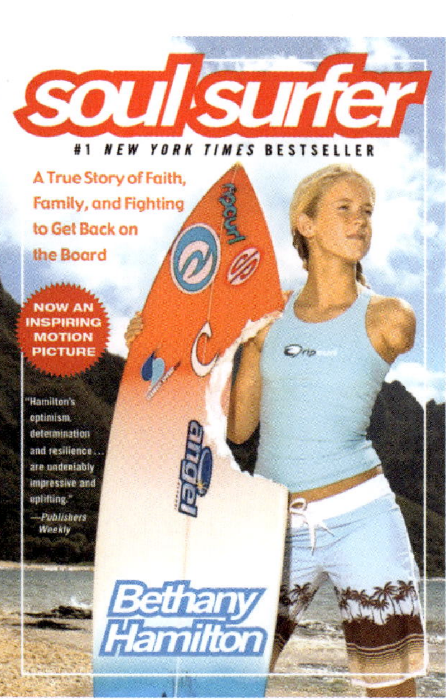

This book cover develops a truly inspiring 'implied **narrative**', or suggested story. We can infer from the image and writing on the cover that Bethany Hamilton was attacked by a shark while surfing and lost her arm as a result. We can draw this conclusion due to the **symbolism** of the large shark bite in the surfboard and Hamilton's missing arm. However, we are also told she has bravely continued to 'get back on the board' when many others may have given up or been too fearful to surf again.

The text represents Hamilton as an inspiration due to her determined, fearless and positive outlook. We are even told that the story has been made into 'an inspiring motion picture' (film).

narrative The selection and sequencing of events or experiences, real or imagined, to tell a story to entertain, engage, inform and extend imagination, typically using an orientation, complication and resolution

symbolism The use of one object, person or situation to signify or represent another, by giving them meanings that are different from their literal sense (e.g. a dove is a symbol of peace)

2.2 Check for understanding

1 Tick the features of the book cover that represent the idea that Hamilton is inspirational.

a Hamilton displays a determined, future-focused facial expression and body language. ☐

b The image shows a beach setting, which looks like fun. ☐

c A reviewer states that Hamilton has admirable qualities such as 'optimism' and 'resilience'. ☐

d The image features Hamilton having a great time with her friends. ☐

e The cover shows how disabilities or physical difference shouldn't stop you from enjoying life. ☐

To 'inspire change' means to motivate a shift or transformation in a person such as:

- an altered opinion, attitude or point of view
- different behaviours or actions
- a commitment to a certain habit or way of thinking.

The book cover and the story within might inspire others to change their attitudes toward the challenges or obstacles they face. They might even be inspired to accept their own physical differences instead of being deterred by them.

Persuasive techniques

Many of the texts that inspire change can be classified as persuasive texts, such as speeches and advertisements. Below is a summary of some common techniques used to inspire change.

Persuasive technique	Explanation
imperatives and calls to action	a direct command or a request – e.g. 'Just do it.'
emotive language or images	deliberately strong words or images that provoke emotion in the reader or viewer – e.g. distressing, emotive scenes in drink-driving advertisements.
inclusive language	using words such as 'we', 'us' and 'our' to make an **audience** feel included in a message – e.g. 'We all have a responsibility to call out bullying when we see it.'
repetition	a word, **phrase** or full sentence that is repeated to emphasise its significance. Repetition of the same words or phrases at the beginning of consecutive sentences is called 'anaphora'.
celebrity appeals	use of well-known public figures and celebrities whom others might idolise or look up to and want to take advice from – e.g. Serena Williams in Nike advertising.

Persuasive technique	Explanation
metaphor and simile	figures of speech that compare two things by suggesting one is the other (metaphor) or one is like the other (simile) – e.g. 'He is a beacon of hope to others.'
appeal to values	targeting the values of an audience. Values are the principles and ideals we believe are important – e.g. an audience may value their family or loyalty.

audience An intended or assumed group of readers, listeners or viewers that a writer, designer, filmmaker or speaker is addressing
phrase A group of words often beginning with a preposition but without a subject and verb combination (e.g. 'on the river'; 'with brown eyes')
metaphor A type of figurative language used to describe a person or object through an implicit comparison to something with similar characteristics
simile A device comparing 2 things that are not alike. Similes use 'like', 'as' or 'than' to make the comparison (e.g. The cake was as light as air)
values Ideas and beliefs specific to individuals and groups

2.3

Check for understanding

1 Identify examples of the following persuasive devices used in this PETA advertisement featuring Kellan Lutz, the actor from the *Twilight* film series.

a imperative ________________________

b emotive image ________________________

c celebrity appeal ________________________

d metaphor ________________________

2 What change is the advertisement trying to inspire?

Scan the QR code to access the advertisement.

Inspirational speeches

Have you heard of Malala Yousafzai? She is a young woman who lived in Pakistan while it was under the strict rule of the Taliban. From the age of eleven, Malala spoke out as an activist for girls' education, which was denied by the Taliban.

When she was 15, Malala was badly injured by a Taliban gunman. She survived the incident and continues to advocate for girls' education. Below is an extract from a speech Malala delivered to the United Nations in 2013.

Dear Friends, on the 9th of October 2012, the Taliban shot me on the left side of my forehead. They shot my friends too. They thought that the bullets would silence us. But they failed. And then, out of that silence came thousands of voices. The terrorists thought that they would change our aims and stop our ambitions but nothing changed in my life except this: weakness, fear and hopelessness died. Strength, power and courage was born. I am the same Malala. My ambitions are the same. My hopes are the same. My dreams are the same.

…

Dear sisters and brothers, we realise the importance of light when we see darkness. We realise the importance of our voice when we are silenced. In the same way, when we were in Swat, the north of Pakistan, we realised the importance of pens and books when we saw the guns. The wise saying, "The pen is mightier than the sword." It is true.

…

We call upon the world leaders that all the peace deals must protect women and children's rights. A deal that goes against the dignity of women and their rights is unacceptable.

We call upon all governments to ensure free compulsory education for every child all over the world.

We call upon all governments to fight against terrorism and violence, to protect children from brutality and harm.

We call upon the developed nations to support the expansion of educational opportunities for girls in the developing world.

We call upon all communities to be tolerant – to reject prejudice based on cast, creed, sect, religion or gender. To ensure freedom and equality for women so that they can flourish. We cannot all succeed when half of us are held back.

We call upon our sisters around the world to be brave – to embrace the strength within themselves and realise their full potential.

…

Dear brothers and sisters, we must not forget that millions of people are suffering from poverty, injustice and ignorance. We must not forget that millions of children are out of schools. We must not forget that our sisters and brothers are waiting for a bright peaceful future.

So let us wage a global struggle against illiteracy, poverty and terrorism and let us pick up our books and pens. They are our most powerful weapons.

2.4 Check for understanding

1 According to Malala, what was the reason for the Taliban shooting her and her friends?

____

____

2 What are the main changes that Malala explains came from the shooting in the first paragraph of the extract?

____

____

3 Malala starts multiple consecutive sentences with the same words: 'We call upon …' Circle the terms below that can be used for this technique. Use a dictionary to help if necessary. There are two correct answers.

anecdote   repetition   anaphora   adjective   conjunction

4 What metaphor does Malala use to end the speech, and what two things is she comparing?

____

____

Speech delivery

Even the most strongly written speech can be destroyed by a poor delivery. Speech delivery can be divided into two main areas: body language and voice.

Body language is important as it can help engage your audience and add impact to the content of your speech. Successful speakers:

- make eye contact with members of the audience
- stand confidently with a straight back and shoulders down
- use appropriate hand gestures to emphasise points.

The volume, pacing and intonation (expression) of your voice are also vital in delivering an engaging speech. Successful speakers:

adjective A word class that describes, identifies or quantifies a noun or a pronoun, e.g. two (number or quantity), my (possessive), ancient (descriptive), shorter (comparative), wooden (classifying)

conjunction In a sentence, a word that joins other words, groups/phrases or clauses together in a logical relationship such as addition, time, cause or comparison. There are 2 types: coordinating and subordinating

» deliver their speech at an appropriate volume and adjust their voice to be louder or quieter for special emphasis
» vary pace for effect and use pauses for impact
» alter the intonation (rise and fall) of their voice so that they don't sound monotonous.

2.5

Check for understanding

In 2014, Malala Yousafzai was awarded a Nobel Peace Prize. Her Nobel Lecture can be viewed via the internet. Watch the speech and tick off the following points of Malala's delivery as you observe them. (If you can't watch Malala's Nobel Lecture, the checklist can be applied to any other speech, including student speeches.)

Techniques of effective speech delivery	Tick if used
makes regular eye contact with members of the audience	
stands confidently with a straight back and shoulders down	
uses appropriate hand gestures	
speaks at an appropriate volume	
speaks at an appropriate pace; uses pause for effect	
alters intonation	

Nominalisation

Nominalisation is the process of turning adjectives or **verbs** into **nouns**. You can transform a verb or an adjective into a noun by adding an appropriate **suffix**. The following are examples.

inspiring (adjective) → inspiration (noun)

introduce (verb) → introduction (noun)

The effect of nominalisation is that instead of describing actions or people, the text is now focused on ideas or concepts. Consider the following sentences.

verb A word class that expresses processes that include doing, feeling, thinking, saying and relating
noun A word class that includes all words denoting person, place, object or thing, idea or emotion. Nouns may be common, proper, collective, abstract and compound
suffix An element added to the end of a word to change its meaning (e.g. to form past tense: '-ed'; to show a smaller amount or degree: -less; to form an adverb: -ly)

» The inspiring student was a role model to her peers. / The student was an inspiration to her peers.
» New scientific evidence was introdvuced and led to … / The introduction of new scientific evidence led to …

Nominalisation can make a text sound formal and factual, therefore nominalisations are often found in texts that use scientific or abstract ideas, such as informative reports and scientific studies. However, they can be found in a range of other texts too, such as those we've looked at in this chapter. In the extract from Malala Yousafzai's UN speech, you can see how she often nominalises the adjective 'important' by changing it to 'importance', as in the line 'we realise the importance of light when we see darkness'.

2.6

Check for understanding

1 Transform the following verbs (v) and adjectives (adj) into nouns.

a investigate (v) ____________________

b intend (v) ____________________

c develop (v) ____________________

d discuss (v) ____________________

e violent (adj) ____________________

f healthy (adj) ____________________

g permanent (adj) ____________________

h difficult (adj) ____________________

2 Rewrite the following sentences, changing the underlined words to phrases using nominalisations – e.g. 'The student questioned how reliable the text was' becomes 'The student questioned the reliability of the text'.

a Chemicals <u>polluting</u> the air are a cause of climate change.

____

b NASA's scientists can <u>observe</u> Earth's changes from space.

____

c We are <u>obliged</u> to <u>protect</u> and <u>preserve</u> the environment.

____

Inspirational songs

Music has a long history of inspiring change in society. You might have heard famous songs like 'Imagine' by John Lennon, 'Don't Worry, Be Happy' by Bobby McFerrin or 'Beautiful' written by Linda Perry and recorded by Christina Aguilera. Songs like these inspire us to change our behaviours or **attitudes.**

attitudes Particular ways of thinking and feeling towards people or things

One song that inspires listeners to reflect on and change their behaviour is 'Proud' by Heather Small, a British soul singer. It was released as her first single and became a worldwide hit, later becoming the official theme song used to promote London in its bid to host the 2012 Olympic Games.

Scan the QR code, or click **here** to access the lyrics.

Heather Small

2.7

Reflecting and discussing

Discuss the following questions in pairs, in small groups or with the whole class as directed by your teacher.

1 Why do you think the song 'Proud' was selected for the 2012 London Olympic Games bid?

2 What words or techniques in the lyrics of 'Proud' inspire people to change? What kind of change is being encouraged?

The music of Baker Boy (Danzal James Baker OAM), rapper, dancer, actor, artist and 2019 Young Australian of the Year, can also be considered very inspiring. Baker Boy's hip-hop songs combine English and Yolngu Matha language to explore Australian culture and identity. Visit the website and explore why song lyrics like 'Black Magic' and 'Marryuna' are so inspiring to listeners.

2.8 Get creative

Write your own inspirational song lyrics based on ONE of the following ideas.

» a song that inspires listeners to treat others with kindness and respect

» a song that inspires listeners to stand up to bullies

» a song that inspires listeners to accept the way they look.

Inspirational images

Images can also inspire us. The image below is the promotional image for the audiobook version of Jessica Watson's biography, *True Spirit*. It tells the amazing story of her solo sailing journey around the world at only 16 years of age. Read the annotations about how the image is constructed to represent the subject as an inspiring person through the implied narrative, or suggested story, that it creates.

The composition includes a vast sunlit ocean, suggesting the power and beauty of nature.

The close-up shot captures the subject's warm, smiling facial expression and gaze directed towards viewers, suggesting she is a friendly and admirable person who is easy to relate to.

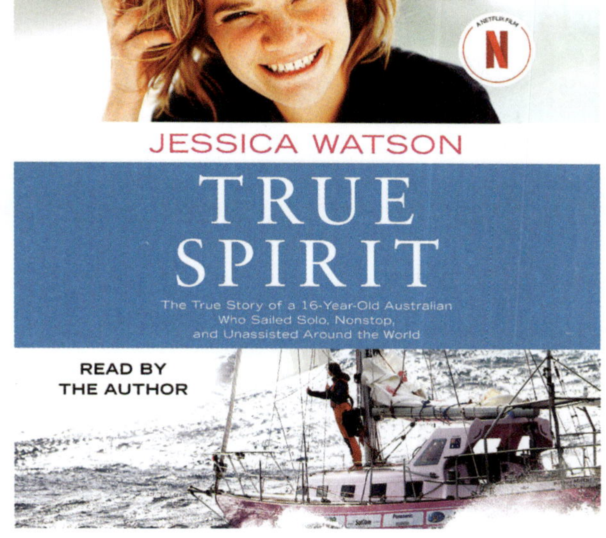

The long shot captures Watson's small boat, dwarfed in size by the swelling wave behind it, adding to the sense of the power and danger of the ocean.

Active body language is shown in the subject grasping the sailing ropes and facing the ocean, suggesting Watson's skill and determination to succeed.

Appeals to values

One of the main ways in which a person or text can inspire us is through an appeal to our values. This means the person or text targets the beliefs, principles or ideals that are particularly important to us.

Lots of people value such principles as freedom, family and an education. Personal qualities like a strong work ethic, kindness or resilience are also valued as important. Not everyone shares the same values, though, and your values can change over your lifetime. Right now, you may value the acceptance and approval of your friends, but later in life you might value your health or job security more.

Look at the following image.

The stated meaning of the image is captured in the written text – 'A dog makes your life happier' – but there is also an 'implied' meaning, or a meaning that is hinted at. This meaning is more subtly suggested by the implied narrative or the 'subtext' created by the image. The implied overall meaning of the advertisement is not only that adopting a dog is a kind and loving thing to do that will bring joy to the dog owner's life, but also that dogs should be fed Pedigree – it is an advertisement, after all!

2.9

Check for understanding

1 Using the Jessica Watson example earlier as a model, annotate the image above, identifying its **visual features** and their implied meanings.

2 What change in the audience is the text trying to inspire? Think about the 'before and after' construction of the advertisement.

____

____

3 Circle the values that you think the advertisement above appeals to or targets.

mental health	determination	kindness
family	financial wealth	animal welfare

visual features Visual components of a text which may include placement, salience, framing, representation of action or reaction, shot size, social distance and camera angle

Fascinating photography

You've probably heard the famous saying 'A picture is worth a thousand words'. But what does it actually mean? It suggests that it would take many pages of writing to convey the same meaning as what can be captured and communicated in a single image such as a painting or a photograph. An understanding of photographs is important in English because we encounter them in advertising, social media, journalism and other texts. This unit is all about appreciating the way in which photographs create meaning and how they can also guide us to form responses or viewpoints.

In this unit you will learn:

- about visual techniques and elements used to create photographs
- how to look closely at a photograph and identify the context it reflects
- how photographs position us to respond to them and to form viewpoints.

Curriculum content

Australian Curriculum content description	Content code
Explain how language and/or images in texts position readers to respond and form viewpoints.	AC9E8LE03
Identify how texts reflect contexts.	AC9E8LY01

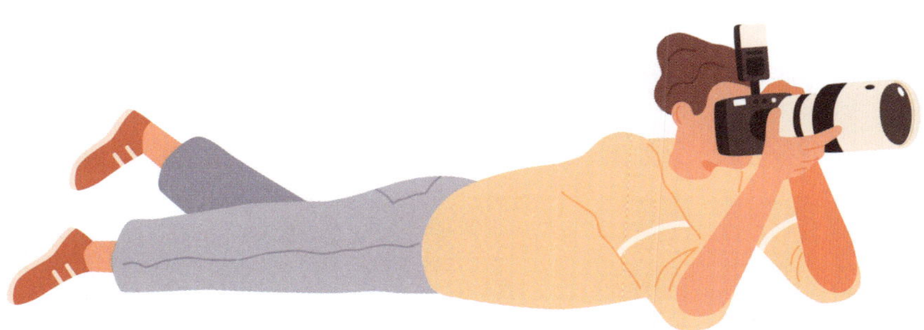

The power of photographs

Photographs shape our reactions to ideas, places and issues by showing us events and the people involved in them. A photograph can help us feel like we are witnessing a scene firsthand.

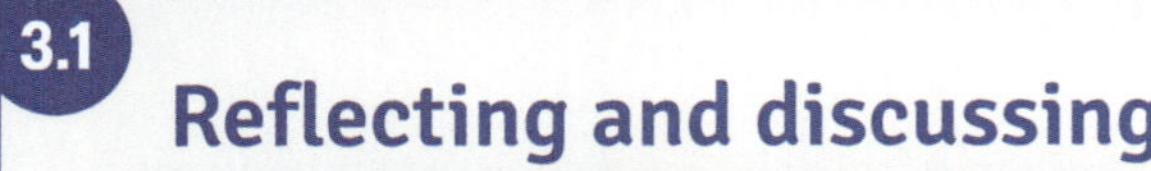

3.1 Reflecting and discussing

What kind of event does this photograph represent? Discuss with a partner and give reasons for your answer.

Visual features

Many visual components or elements are used in the creation of photographs and other images. We call these visual features. The main **visual features** are:

visual features Visual components of a text which may include placement, salience, framing, representation of action or reaction, shot size, social distance and camera angle

salience A strategy of emphasis, highlighting what is important in a text. In images, it is achieved through strategies such as the placement of an item in the foreground, size and contrast in tone or colour

symbolism The use of one object, person or situation to signify or represent another, by giving them meanings that are different from their literal sense (e.g. a dove is a symbol of peace)

3.2 Check for understanding

Match the visual features below with their definitions by drawing a connecting line between them. You may need to use a process of elimination, work together with others, or refer to a dictionary when deciding on the answers. Some answers have been done for you.

Visual feature	Definitions
symbols	emphasis on a certain part of an image, achieved through size, contrast in tone or colour, placing something in the foreground etc.
composition	the way elements in an image are enclosed by its borders, including how much setting is included or elements that are partially cut out of the image
salience	the object or person captured in the image; can also refer to what the image is about or its 'subject matter'
framing	lines that aid direction and movement; sometimes also called leading lines because they lead the viewer's eyes to a particular point in the image
shot size	how things are arranged and where they are placed within the frame. Includes consideration of symmetry and balance, as well as what has been placed in the foreground, mid-ground and background
camera angle	the degree of closeness or distance between the subject and the viewer, which can determine the connection we feel to the subject, making us comfortable, uncomfortable, etc.
social distance	the positioning of the camera to capture the subject. The camera may be positioned looking up at something, looking down on it, at the same height as the viewer, from a side angle, etc.
vectors	how close or far away the camera is how much of the subject or setting is included in the shot, such as an extreme close-up or a long shot
subject	signs or objects used to represent something else, such as a rose to represent romance or the colour red to symbolise danger

3.3 Reflecting and discussing

Discuss the following questions in pairs, in small groups or with the whole class as directed by your teacher.

1 What is the subject matter of the photograph above? What is it about?
2 What degree of social distance is created by the image? Do you think it creates a close connection between the people and you as a viewer, or a distant, remote one? Give reasons for your answer.
3 How do you respond to the photograph? Try to explain the emotions or sensations you feel when looking at it.

Candid photographs

Candid photographs are those where the subject has not posed or been arranged in a particular way. A candid photograph might capture events or people mid-action when they don't even know they are being photographed. For this reason, candid photographs can sometimes seem more genuine and natural compared to photographs that are staged.

3.4 Check for understanding

Which of these two photographs do you think is candid? Provide reasons for your answer, comparing the visual features of the images.

Photograph A

Photograph B

____

____

____

____

Understanding the effects of visual features

Sometimes we can't be certain whether a photograph is candid or not. It might not look set up or posed, even if it is, because the photographer was deliberately trying to create the effect of looking natural. There are many other effects that might be created by a photograph's visual features and the specific techniques used to create the photograph.

3.5

Check for understanding

Draw lines between each of the visual features or techniques below and the effect that they are likely to produce.

Visual features and techniques	Definitions
a high camera angle looking down on a tiny subject	can lead the viewer's eye to the background of the image where there may be an important detail
an extreme close-up shot on a person's eyes, with tears welling in them	image may seem slightly blurred; can suggest nostalgia, sentimentality or romance
a soft-focus filter or lens	can create a satisfying sense of symmetry and balance; makes the centre subject salient
a wide shot that captures lots of people crowded together	can make the subject appear vulnerable, dominated or submissive
a railway line heading into the distance	can capture an important human emotion, such as sadness; can invite empathy
an image where the subject is centred and surrounded by the same objects on either side	can create a sense of claustrophobia or chaos; may also evoke a sense of energetic excitement and human connection

Look at the photograph below and read the annotations about the visual features and their effects.

A Long shot captures the wide landscape of the scene, having the effect of making the setting look open and inviting.

Salience of the central, mid-ground subject has the effect of highlighting the importance of the relationship between humans and nature.

Framing includes the sun rising over the distant mountains, producing the effect that light pours over the natural landscape, making it look beautiful and striking.

The overall effect of the photograph's visual features is to produce an **aesthetically** pleasing, picturesque image that shows the beauty of the natural world, encouraging viewers to appreciate and enjoy it for themselves.

aesthetic Concerned with a sense of beauty or an appreciation of artistic expression

3.6

Check for understanding

1 Look closely at the photograph below. Using the previous example as a model, write your own annotations about the effects created by various visual features.

2 Summarise the overall effect of the photograph's visual features.

Curated photographs

The word 'curate' means to carefully choose or organise something for presentation. Curated photographs, then, are the ones that we might deliberately set up, manipulate or pose for.

Do you ever crop a photograph before deciding on a final version to send to a friend? Have you ever applied a filter to a photo before posting it to social media? Do you ever change your clothes, hair or even facial expressions for photographs? If you answered 'Yes' to any of these questions, then you are already curating your own photographs.

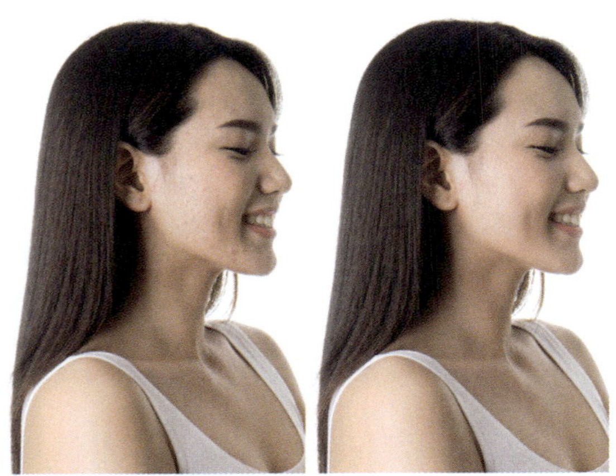

Look at the two images of the same person below. Both of them have been curated, but the image on the right is a digitally altered version of the image on the left.

3.7

Reflecting and discussing

Discuss the following questions in pairs, in small groups or with the whole class, as directed by your teacher.

1 What are the changes can you see between the two photographs?
2 What would be the reason for digitally altering a photograph?
3 Where might curated photographs be seen in everyday life?

Filters and cropping are frequently used techniques in the curation of photographs. The images below are three versions of the same photograph. Differences between them are created using:

- composition
- a colour filter.
- cropping

Image 1

Image 2

Image 3

3.8

Check for understanding

Complete the analytical sentences about each photograph in the spaces below. The sentences will guide you to think about the effects of the visual features and techniques used in the curation of each image. The first one has been done for you as an example.

1 Image 1:

The colours that dominate Image 1 are the brown of the road, the green of the grass and the bright blue of the sky. Together with the composition placing the truck at a distance within a wide, spacious scene, this makes the setting seem isolated and remote. The bright yellow of the truck in the background also stands out because it seems out of place in the landscape.

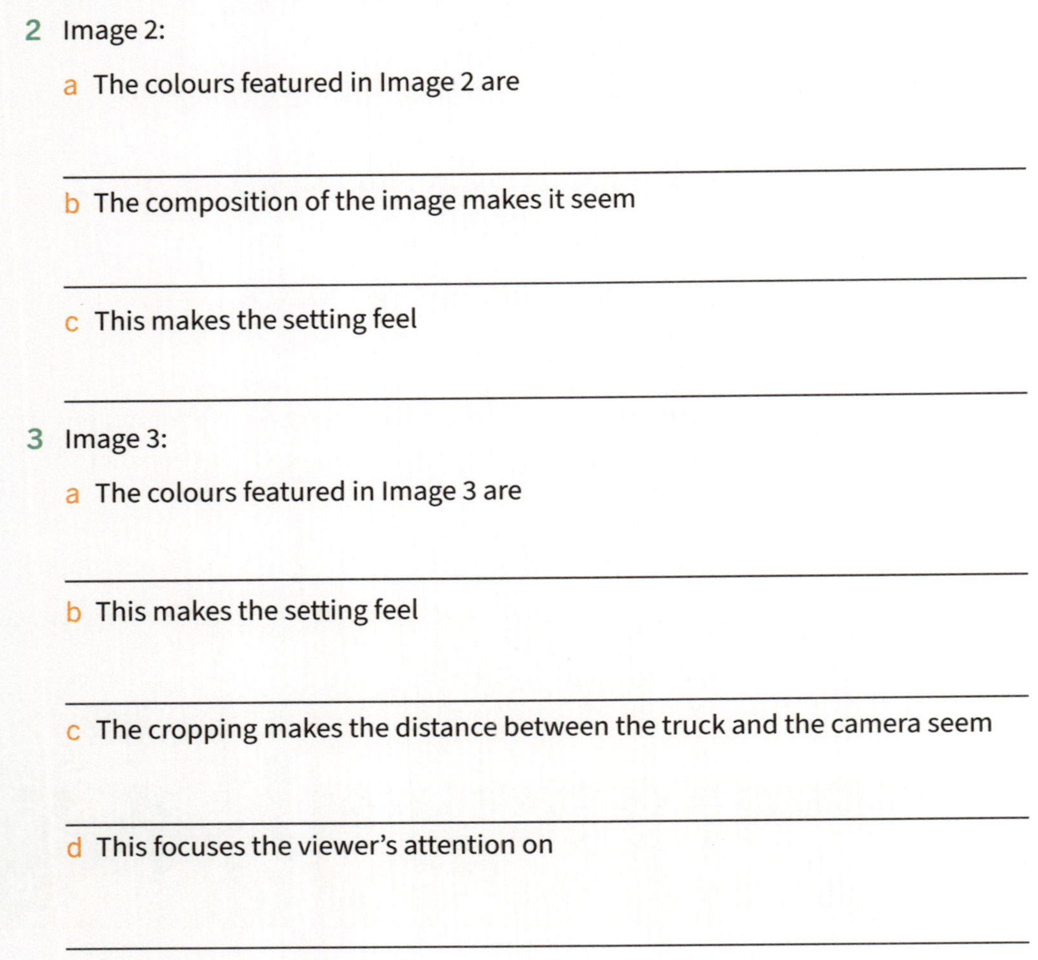

2 Image 2:

a The colours featured in Image 2 are

____

b The composition of the image makes it seem

____

c This makes the setting feel

____

3 Image 3:

a The colours featured in Image 3 are

____

b This makes the setting feel

____

c The cropping makes the distance between the truck and the camera seem

____

d This focuses the viewer's attention on

____

The reality is that even seemingly spontaneous, candid photographs are still curated in some way. Even if a subject doesn't know they are being photographed and they are captured in a very natural-looking way, the photographer still has to make decisions about:

» what to include in the frame when taking the photograph
» what to leave out of the frame when taking the photograph
» whether to crop out part of the scene after the photograph has been taken
» what angle to take the shot from
» how close to get to the subject when taking the photograph
» whether to use a soft focus or a filter on the photograph.

Understanding these choices might help you to draw some conclusions about how a photographer wants the viewer to respond to the photograph.

3.9 Reflecting and discussing

Discuss the following questions in pairs, in small groups or with the whole class, as directed by your teacher.

1 What was the last photo you took?
2 What decisions from the list above did you have to make?
3 What response to the photo were you aiming for?

Positioning viewers: emotions and viewpoints

Whether deliberately or not, photographs position us to respond in a particular way. Possible responses to a photograph might be emotions or feelings such as:

interest	discomfort	motivation	curiosity	appreciation	respect

Another way of responding to a photograph can be to think a certain way or form a viewpoint about the subject matter. A viewpoint is a way of seeing something or an opinion about something. Look at this photograph and the summary of the emotions and viewpoint it positions viewers to form.

Emotional responses:

The kind gesture of the soldier giving fruit to the children may position viewers to respond with respect and admiration to this action. They may respond with compassion or sympathy for the children, as the mid shot emphasises their small size and vulnerability relative to the soldier they look up at.

Viewpoint:

The audience may form the viewpoint that the soldier, and perhaps the military generally, has a kind-hearted and compassionate nature, even though the job may involve violence and mental toughness. The viewpoint that the soldier is on an admirable peace-keeping mission might be formed.

audience An intended or assumed group of readers, listeners or viewers that a writer, designer, filmmaker or speaker is addressing

3.10 Check for understanding

Using the previous example as a model, explain how the photograph below positions viewers to respond and form a viewpoint.

Emotional responses:

Viewpoint:

3.11 Get creative

Take or find three photographs. Place them in the spaces provided and identify what emotional responses and viewpoints you believe they invite from viewers.

Photograph 1

Emotional responses:

Viewpoint:

Photograph 2

Emotional responses:

Viewpoint:

Photograph 3

Emotional responses:

Viewpoint:

Identifying context

Analysing visual features will also help you to understand how a photograph reflects a particular context. For example, you might know that a photograph was taken a long time ago, in an historical context, if it is black and white or in a sepia (reddish-brown) tone and the subjects are dressed in old-fashioned clothing. You might recognise the Australian context of a photograph if it includes national landmarks or native animals. The images we find in the news often inform us about issues happening in a particular place and time, therefore exposing us to a certain context. In all these examples, you are reading the visual language in order to identify the photograph's context.

context An environment or situation (social, cultural or historical) in which a text is responded to or created. Or wording surrounding an unfamiliar word, which a reader or listener uses to understand its meaning

UNIT 4

Making connections

Have you ever read a story that reminds you of one you've read before? Or have you watched a funny film that imitates the plot or characters from other films? What about viewing a film version of a novel? This unit is all about the ways we make connections between texts. It will explain how we use our prior experiences of other stories to make sense of new or unfamiliar ones. The unit will also help you to recognise that some authors deliberately connect to other texts through direct quotation, allusion, parody and adaptation. Other times, the connections between texts may be less intentional and only evident due to the way we read them.

In this unit you will learn:

- about intertextuality
- to practise making connections between texts
- to explore how layers of meaning can be created.

Curriculum content

Australian Curriculum content description	Content code
Investigate how visual texts use intertextual references to enhance and layer meaning.	AC9E8LA07
Identify intertextual references in literary texts and explain how the references enable new understanding of the aesthetic quality of the text.	AC9E8LE04

What is intertextuality?

'Intertextuality' is the word that we give to a process of making **intertextual references** or connections between different texts. It is when a creator of a text, either deliberately or unconsciously, connects their composition to other texts. They might quote a famous line from another text, create a spin-off using an established character, or adapt a novel into a film.

The term 'intertextuality' also refers to a reading practice in which we draw on our knowledge of other texts to understand a new one. For example, if you read a short story, you will naturally expect that it will include conventions from other short stories you have read, like characters, settings and a plot. If the story is science fiction, you might recognise familiar features of a science fiction film you have watched.

intertextual references associations or connections between one text and other texts that may be overt or less explicit. They can take the form of direct quotation, parody, allusion or structural borrowing

4.1 Reflecting and discussing

Discuss the following questions in pairs, in small groups or with the whole class, as directed by your teacher.

1 Have a close look at the image above, which includes characters from the animated film *Shrek*. Do they remind you of the characters from other texts? Which other texts?

2 What is common to all of the texts that these characters come from? Think about the genre they all belong to.

Connecting through questioning

The following diagram shows the types of questions that you can ask yourself when trying to make intertextual connections between texts.

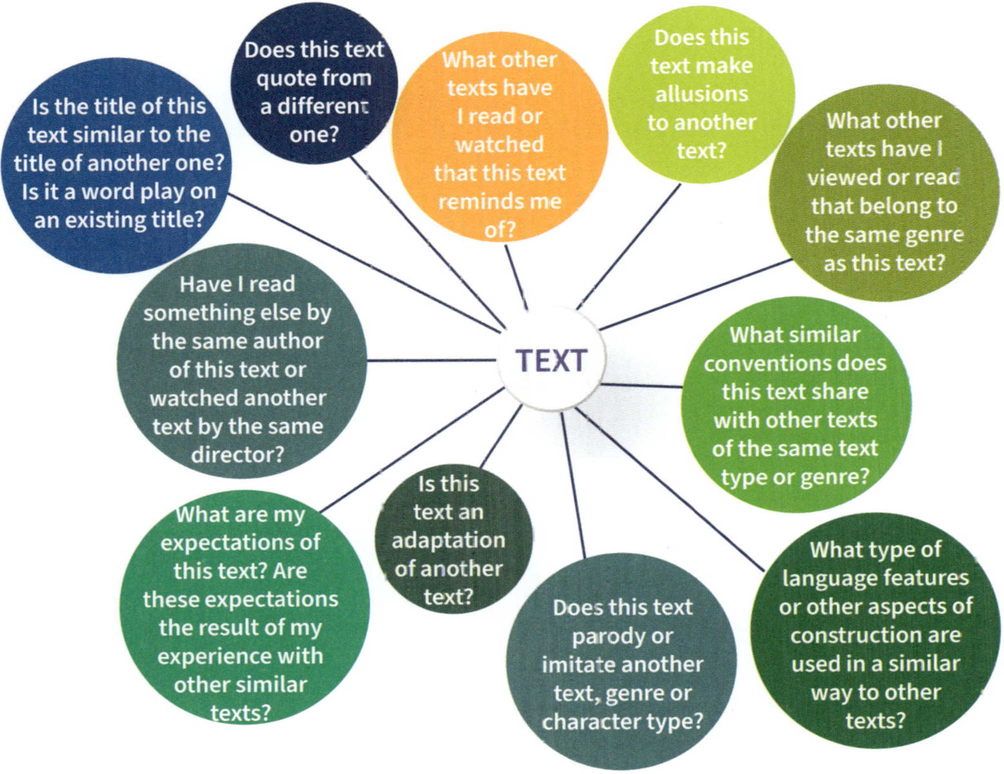

4.2 Check for understanding

1 Select a text that you have recently read or viewed and write the title of it below.

____

2 Select two questions from the diagram above that you can answer in full sentences with reference to this text. Record the questions and your answers to them in the spaces provided.

a question: ______________________________

____

answer: ______________________________

____

b question: ______________________________

____

answer: ______________________________

____

Types of intertextuality

Intertextuality can take many forms, including direct quotation, parody, allusion and adaptation. Have a look at the following definitions and the examples provided

Look at the table below that illustrates the differences between personal and social identities.

Type of intertextuality	Definition	Examples
direct quotation	reusing another author's or person's words that a reader will recognise, such as quoting a well-known line from a novel or play	'Call me Ishmael' is the first line of the famous novel *Moby Dick* and is quoted in the opening and final lines of the novel *Don't Call Me Ishmael* by Michael Gerard Bauer.
parody	an exaggerated imitation or spoof of another text or genre for comic effect	*Hotel Transylvania* is a comedy film parody of the story of Count Dracula.
allusion	an indirect reference or hint to a person, character, event, idea or text	'Her nose will soon be as long as Pinocchio's if she keeps lying' or 'Chocolate cake is my Achilles heel' are examples.
adaptation	changing or remaking a text by recreating it in a different way, such as adapting a novel for the stage or screen	The novel *Matilda* has been adapted into a stage musical, a radio program and two films.

4.3

Check for understanding

Using the definitions and examples above to help you, decide whether the descriptions below could be considered direct quotations, parodies, allusions or adaptations. Write your answers in the spaces.

a The novel *Charlie and the Chocolate Factory* has been made into two films.

____

b He's acting like a lovesick Romeo. ______________________________

c *Enchanted* is a film that pokes fun at the fairytale genre by exaggerating how unrealistic the plot lines and characters are. ______________________________

d 'Then leaf subsides to leaf. So Eden sank to grief' (from 'Nothing Gold Can Stay' by Robert Frost) ______________________________

e *Little Women*, a novel by Louisa May Alcott, was made into a film in 2019.

____

Layers of meaning

Reading or creating intertextual connections can have the effect of enhancing meaning or adding layers of meaning to a text. This could be achieved by developing a particular **theme**, offering a new perspective on a topic, or challenging the representation offered in another text.

theme The main idea, concept or message of a text

4.4 Check for understanding

Read the stanza from the famous Australian poem 'My Country' in the left-hand column below, then read the right-hand version'

Stanza from 'My Country' by Dorothea Mackellar	Stanza from Oscar Krahnvohl's version of the poem
I love a sunburnt country, A land of sweeping plains, Of ragged mountain ranges, Of droughts and flooding rains. I love her far horizons, I love her jewel-sea, Her beauty and her terror – The wide brown land for me!	I love a sunburnt country, A land of open drains Mid-urban sprawl expanded For cost-accounting gains; Broad, busy bulldozed acres Once wastes of fern and trees Now rapidly enriching Investors overseas.

1 What aspects of the Australian country does Dorothea Mackellar love, according to the poem?

___

___

___

2 Mackellar's poem includes many contrasting descriptions. Tick the elements below that are contrasted by Mackellar

a ragged mountains and big hills ☐
b droughts and flooding ☐
c beauty and terror ☐
d jewel-sea and crystal waters ☐
e wide and narrow land ☐
f sunburn and frostbite ☐

3 What is the effect of calling Australia 'her' in the poem?

___

___

4 Now read the stanza in the right-hand column of the table again. What features in it help you understand its intertextual connection to Dorothea Mackellar's original poem?

____

____

5 What comment is Oscar Krahnvohl making about Australia in his poem?

____

____

Contexts and intertextuality

Sometimes the creators of texts will update the representations of people, ideas and events from older stories to reflect modern, changed contexts. A good example of this is fairytales. These stories were once communicated in oral form until they were then written down by authors like Charles Perrault, Hans Christian Andersen and the Grimm Brothers in the eighteenth and nineteenth centuries. From the 1920s onwards, many of the stories were then adapted by Disney for young audiences.

Early versions of fairytales commonly represent ways of thinking about the world that we might now consider dated and old-fashioned. For example, in the Disney versions of 'Cinderella' and 'Rapunzel', the main female characters are both saved from their miserable lives by a handsome, heroic prince. The characters are depicted as 'damsels in distress', an archetype (common character type). Modern adaptations of fairytales, however, challenge these plot lines and character tropes to reflect changing attitudes, behaviours and values in our society.

4.5 Reflecting and discussing

Discuss the following questions in pairs, in small groups or with the whole class as directed by your teacher.

"Your carriage awaits"

1 What fairytales do the images above make intertextual connections to?

2 What features have been added to the images to reflect a modern context?

Fractured fairytales

'Fractured fairytales' are a type of parody that change the classic versions of texts to offer a modern twist to them. They rely on readers' understanding of the original versions of fairytales to add another layer of meaning to the narrative. Fractured fairytales often reflect modern contexts by updating characters, plots and settings.

For instance, instead of reproducing the 'damsel in distress' archetype, a fractured fairytale might represent a female character as the brave hero who saves a man, or it may represent a female as independent and in no need of a man for happiness at all.

4.6

Check for understanding

OF COURSE you think Goldilocks was a brat who broke in and trashed our house. You don't know the other side of the story. Well, let me tell you ...

This fractured fairytale provides a fresh perspective on a well-known tale.

1 Look at the front cover of the novel above and read its promotional blurb.

a What original fairytale does the book connect to?

____

b What elements of the original story do you think might be changed in this new version to provide a 'fresh perspective'?

____

____

The candy recipes of the goody shops have been stolen by the Goody Bandit, and many animals are out of business. While the police are chasing the criminal, there is a mess at Granny's house involving Little Red Riding Hood, The Wolf, The Woodsman and Granny, disturbing the peace in the forest. They are all arrested by the impatient Chief Grizzly...

2 Look at the film poster above and read its promotional blurb.

a What original fairytale does the film connect to?

____

b What elements of the original story do you think might be changed in this new version to make it an 'irrepressible' retelling?

____

____

4.7 Get creative

Choose a fairytale that you are familiar with and rewrite it as a fractured fairytale by updating and changing its setting, plot or characters. Here are some ideas:

- Rewrite 'Cinderella' as an action story in which Cinderella is a secret agent infiltrating the palace.
- Rewrite 'Little Red Riding Hood' as a comedy in which Red Riding Hood keeps chasing the wolf because she wants to keep him as her pet.

Visual intertextuality

Advertisers and the creators of television programs and films sometimes make visual intertextual connections very purposefully. For instance, the advertisement displayed here is for Movember, an annual public fundraising initiative that aims to bring attention to men's health issues by encouraging them to grow a moustache throughout November.

The image references familiar fairytale plots, setting and characters, where the heroic man on horseback saves or romances a beautiful woman. By presenting these elements in visual form and linking them to the written text 'Be a Hero', the advertisement playfully suggests that men who participate in Movember will be regarded as attractive and heroic by women.

The television program *The Simpsons* is well known for its intertextual approach. For example, one episode is called 'Bart of Darkness', connecting it to the famous novel called *Heart of Darkness. The Simpsons* has referenced many other texts too, including the poem 'The Raven' by Edgar Allen Poe, 'Tom and Jerry' cartoons, and the film *2001: A Space Odyssey.*

4.8 Reflecting and discussing

Discuss the following questions in pairs, in small groups or with the whole class as directed by your teacher

1. How have the artists responsible for the second and third artworks above made intertextual connections to the famous painting *The Mona Lisa* by Leonardo da Vinci (the first image)?
2. What do you think is the purpose of playing with the original artwork in this manner?
3. Apart from the examples from *The Simpsons* mentioned above, what other visual texts like films or television programs, use an intertextual approach like this?

Adaptations

The process of adapting a novel, story, comic or play into a film requires making some careful decisions. The screenwriter and director must choose what to include and what to leave out, how to represent well-known characters and places, and how faithful they will be to the original work. An extra level of complexity is added with adaptations because audiences might know and love the original. There is always a risk that fans of the original text might be disappointed in how the characters, setting and story have been represented.

4.9 Reflecting and discussing

Discuss the following questions in pairs, in small groups or with the whole class, as directed by your teacher.

1. Which of the following film adaptations have you seen? The creator of the original text is added in brackets after each.

The Harry Potter series (JK Rowling), *The BFG* (Roald Dahl),
Coraline (Neil Gaiman), *The Hunger Games series* (Suzanne Collins),
Ant-Man (Stan Lee), *Matilda* (Roald Dahl), *The Divergent series* (Veronica Roth),
Diary of a Wimpy Kid series (Jeff Kinney)

2. Do you think the original versions or the adaptations of the texts are better? Give reasons for your answers.

Case study: The Princess Bride

The Princess Bride is a 1987 American film based on the 1973 novel of the same name by William Goldman. Directed by Rob Reiner, this film is a combination of comedy, adventure, romance and fantasy. This type of film is a spoof – a funny, mocking imitation. Watch the first 15 minutes of *The Princess Bride* or watch the trailer, freely available on YouTube.

4.10

Check for understanding

1 How do you think the story will be presented in the film?

a as a realistic narrative ☐

b as a book being read by a grandfather to a sick grandson ☐

c from the perspective of the princess ☐

2 What are your expectations of this film? What do you think will happen?

____

____

3 What characters are introduced? Describe three of them.

____

____

____

4 Are there any signs that the story might not follow the conventions, or typical features, of a fairytale for children?

____

____

4.11

Get creative

Think of a book that you enjoyed and would like to see turned into a film. Imagine your class is a group of high-powered film studio executives. Write and deliver a two-minute 'pitch' to convince them that the book you have chosen should be made into a film. In your pitch, answer the following questions.

1 Why would the story translate well to the screen?

2 Who would you cast in the lead roles? Why would these actors suit the characters in the film?

3 Who would want to watch the film? Explain why people would flock to the cinema to see this film.

Remember: your aim is to convince them of the brilliance (and moneymaking potential) of your vision for the film. Be enthusiastic and inspiring in your delivery.

Personal writing

Do you ever write about what's happening in your life – maybe in a personal diary or in the form of a social media update? For centuries, people have used diaries to record the private details of their lives, often as a way of making sense of daily events. In the twenty-first century, writers often choose to express their thoughts in online blogs rather than in handwritten diaries, due to the interactive nature of online texts. This unit will help you to understand the ways in which an individual's points of view and values, as well as their relationships and roles, are represented through various forms of personal writing. We will also look at the effects of various language features, including sentence patterns and clause structures.

In this unit you will learn:

- about different forms of personal writing
- to recognise the ways in which ideas and points of view may represent the values of individuals
- how language features create meaning and effect.

Curriculum content

Australian Curriculum content description	Content code
Recognise how language shapes relationships and roles.	AC9E8LA01
Examine a variety of clause structures including embedded clauses that add information and expand ideas in sentences.	AC9E8LA05
Explain the ways that ideas and points of view may represent the values of individuals and groups in literary texts, drawn from historical, social and cultural contexts, by First Nations Australian, and wide-ranging Australian and world authors.	AC9E8LE01
Analyse how language features such as sentence patterns create tone, and literary devices such as imagery create meaning and effect.	AC9E8LE05
Analyse how authors organise ideas to develop and shape meaning.	AC9E8LY04

Types of personal writing

Personal writing can take many different forms including those listed below. All of these text types have something in common: they are a reflective, personal form of writing. They typically include anecdotes, first-person pronouns and recounts of real events from the writer's life using descriptive language.

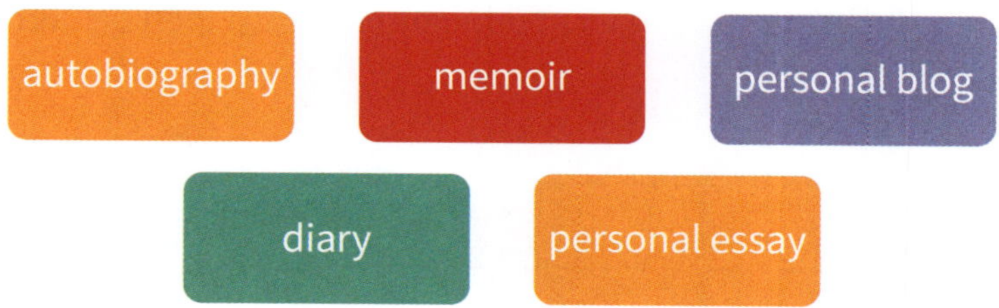

5.1

Check for understanding

1 Which of the types of personal writing above have you ever written or read?

____

2 Record definitions for the following terms.

a anecdotes ______________________________

b first-person pronouns ______________________________

c descriptive language ______________________________

d points of view and values ______________________________

Personal writing allows an author to reflect on and communicate what's really important to them, such as their **values** and points of view. Some commonly held values are honesty, respect and freedom. In this **context**, points of view are the opinions or perspectives presented in a text. For instance, an author may express the point of view that overcoming a tough challenge has made them a stronger person.

values Ideas and beliefs specific to individuals and groups
context An environment or situation (social, cultural or historical) in which a text is responded to or created. Or wording surrounding an unfamiliar word, which a reader or listener uses to understand its meaning

Autobiographical writing

An autobiography tells the story of the writer's own life. Autobiographical writing usually includes recounts from the author's life written in past **tense** and chronological order. Autobiographies can be book-length texts or they can be in the form of shorter recollections.

tense The form a verb takes to signal the location of a clause in time (e.g. present tense 'has' in 'Jo has a cat' locates the situation in the present; past tense 'had' in 'Jo had a cat' locates it in the past)

5.2

Check for understanding

1 Record the titles of some famous Australian autobiographies. You may need to conduct some research.

____

____

2 Research the difference between an autobiography and a memoir. Record the differences below.

____

____

3 Add to the list of **conventions** (typical features) of autobiographies below:

- past tense
- chronological order
- ____________
- ____________

The extract below is from a piece of autobiographical writing titled 'My story' by Alicia Bates. It is a chapter in an anthology of personal writing titled *Growing Up Aboriginal in Australia.*

convention An accepted practice that has developed over time and is generally used and understood (e.g. use of punctuation)

Born in 1989 in Warrnambool, Victoria, on Peek Whurrong-Gunditjmara country, I was my parents' first child and lucky enough to be the first grandchild born on both sides of the family. This meant I had many significant and close relationships with my extended family, being spoilt by my great-grandmother Ma (Dad's nanna), Nanna (Mum's mum), and my uncles and aunties. During the first five years of my life, my parents bought their first home together in Portland, where my dad was a shift worker at the smelter.

Growing up I was always told I was Aboriginal – or Koori, as I prefer; I was always proud of this fact, my country and my people. However, growing up without my father made it difficult to connect with my culture and my people. Often our Koori groups both inside and out of school contained a lot of activities originating from white European culture – or team sports, which I loathed. Having a lighter skin tone, I have been told by others, both Koori and non-Indigenous, that I am 'too white to be Aboriginal' and that I have 'more white blood than black blood'. Last I checked, my blood was red just like everybody else's, and I'm not sure when exactly or how these people measured how much 'black' was in my blood. Furthermore, I have learnt through speaking with many respected elders in our community that our people should not be judged for – or by – the colour of our skin.

When I reflect on what being Aboriginal means for me personally, I know this means: being strong and proud, having a strong connection to my home country and its culture and history, caring for others, my family and community, and having respect for my elders. #Define Aboriginal.

5.3

Check for understanding

1 Circle the values below that Bates communicates in her autobiographical writing. Consider what principles or ideals seem to be most important to her.

fame and fortune	social status	family
culture and history	peace	respect

2 Provide evidence from the text that represents one of these values.

____

____

3 Tick which of the following points of view are represented in the extract.

a People shouldn't be judged by their skin colour. ☐

b Team sports are the best. ☐

c Family is important in shaping a person's identity or sense of self. ☐

d Judging people on their appearance is just a part of life. ☐

e Connection to home country and its culture and history is a part of Bates' identity. ☐

Relationships and roles

The language choices in autobiographical writing can tell us about a person's relationships with others and their role within certain social and cultural groups, or within society more broadly. For instance, in the extract from 'My story', Bates uses lots of naming language and pronouns to locate her role within her own extended family and within the wider community. Re-read the extract, noting where the author names a place, person or group.

The repeated words 'Koori' and 'Aboriginal' in the extract also show Bates' sense of solidarity with and belonging to a certain cultural group. She explains that although her role as a member of this cultural group has been questioned by others, she is confident in her identity.

5.4

Check for understanding

1 Highlight all of the first-person pronouns used in the 'My story' extract. First-person pronouns include 'I', 'me', 'my', 'myself', 'we' and 'our'.

2 What do you think is the effect of this frequent use of first-person pronouns?

____

____

3 In the extract, Bates writes that she prefers the term 'Koori' to the term 'Aboriginal. What is the definition of the word Koori?

____

____

4 What might be a reason for Bates preferring the word Koori?

____

____

5 Find an example from the extract where Bates shows the way language shapes our roles and relationships. Consider her role within her family or a larger cultural group, and her relationships with others in her family and community.

____

____

____

Diary entries

A diary (or journal) is a personal record of day-to-day thoughts and events. It is usually handwritten and divided into separate entries under dates.

A diary or journal is mostly kept private so that the writer is the only one who will ever read it. This means the writer doesn't need to filter their thoughts or edit their experiences – as long as they're confident that their diary won't fall into the wrong hands, they can write whatever they want and not worry about offending anyone.

Some people write as if they're talking to their future self, some address their entries to the diary itself ('Dear Diary'), and others use the diary as an imaginary friend in whom they can confide.

5.5 Reflecting and discussing

Discuss the following questions in pairs, in small groups or with the whole class, as directed by your teacher.

1 What do you think the **purpose** of a personal diary is if no one will ever read it?

2 What sort of things have you written/would you write about in a personal diary?

purpose An intended or assumed reason for a type of text

One of the most famous examples of a personal diary, which was discovered and then published worldwide, is the diary written by Anne Frank. Frank was a German-born Jewish teenager who lived in Amsterdam in the Netherlands with her family during World War II. Frank and her family were forced to go into hiding during the Holocaust (the mass murder of Jewish people under the German Nazi regime during World War II). She wrote her diary, which she called 'Kitty', while she and her family were confined in a secret annexe for two years. She and the others living there were eventually arrested and sent to Nazi concentration camps. Frank died in the Bergen-Belsen concentration camp at the age of 15.

Read the following extract from Anne Frank: *The Diary of a Young Girl*, first published in 1947.

Saturday, 15 July 1944

'Deep down the young are lonelier than the old.' I read this in a book somewhere and it's stuck in my mind. As far as I can tell, it's true. So if you're wondering whether it's harder for the adults here than for the children, the answer is no, it's certainly not. Older people have an opinion about everything and are sure of themselves and their actions. It's twice as hard for us young people to hold on to our opinions at a time when ideals are being shattered and destroyed, when the worst side of human nature predominates, when everyone has come to doubt truth, justice and God. Anyone who claims that the old people have a more difficult time in the Annexe doesn't realise that the problems have a far greater impact on us. We're much too young to deal with these problems, but they keep thrusting themselves on us until, finally, we're forced to think up a solution, though most of the time our solutions crumble when faced with the facts. It's difficult in times like these: ideals, dreams and cherished hopes rise within us, only to be crushed by grim reality. It's a wonder I haven't abandoned all my ideals, they seem so absurd and impractical. Yet I cling to them because I still believe, in spite of everything, that people are truly good at heart.

5.6 Check for understanding

1 Provide a definition for the word 'annexe' ______

2 Anne Frank uses the literary device of **imagery** to create interesting effects and meaning. What is the meaning and effect of each of the following examples of imagery? The first example has been done for you.

Example of imagery	Meaning and effects
'ideals are being shattered and destroyed'	emphasises the permanent destruction and damage to basic human standards; gives insight to the mental impact on Anne and others; invites readers to reflect on their own ideals and beliefs.
'our solutions crumble when faced with the facts'	
'ideals, dreams and cherished hopes rise within us'	
'only to be crushed by grim reality'	

3 Summarise Anne Frank's point of view about what makes the experience of hiding in the annexe more difficult for children than for adults.

______

______

4 Why do you think Anne Frank's diary continues to be so popular with readers today?

______

______

______

imagery Visually descriptive or figurative language to represent things including objects, actions and ideas in ways that appeal to the senses of the reader or viewer

Voice and tone

The **voice** of a piece of personal writing tells the reader about the writer's personality. A writer's voice is uniquely their own. It reflects the way the writer looks at the world.

What do they notice? Which words do they choose to describe it? What thoughts are in their head? Do they write things sarcastically, excitedly or thoughtfully?

Do they use very long sentences, or short ones with exclamation marks, or a mixture of both? These sentence patterns help to create a certain personality, voice and **tone**. For instance, in autobiographical writing, long, detailed sentences can create a thoughtful, reflective tone. **Adjectives** are very useful in describing the tone in a piece of writing. Some examples are:

voice The distinct personality of a piece of writing; the individual writing style of the composer, created through the way they use and mix various language features (e.g. a narrative using a child's voice)
tone The mood created by the language features used by an author and the way the text makes the reader feel
adjective A word class that describes, identifies or quantifies a noun or a pronoun, e.g. two (number or quantity), my (possessive), ancient (descriptive), shorter (comparative), wooden (classifying)

5.7

Check for understanding

1 What sort of person do you think Anne Frank was, based on the voice of her diary?

a thoughtful and hopeful ☐
b pessimistic and angry ☐
c frank and honest ☐
d idealistic and optimistic ☐

2 Sentence patterns can help to create a certain tone. What do you notice about the length of sentences in Anne Frank's diary?

____

3 What effect does the length of the sentences have on Anne Frank's tone in the extract?

____

____

5.8

Get creative

1 Think about your unique **perspective** on the world. Anne Frank was a young, idealistic girl caught up in the middle of a world war. What is it about you, your life experiences and your unique voice that could interest an **audience**?

____

____

2 Now reflect on something in your life right now and write a short diary entry about it in your English notebook.

Blog posts

Blogs are a type of diary for the twenty-first century. The word 'blog' is a shortened version of 'web log'. Blogs are not always private and have the potential to be viewed by enormous numbers of people worldwide who can then respond with comments.

perspective A lens through which the author perceives the world and creates a text, or the lens through which the reader or viewer perceives the world and understands a text

audience An intended or assumed group of readers, listeners or viewers that a writer, designer, filmmaker or speaker is addressing

There are millions of blogs on topics as varied as travel, fashion and politics. If you're interested in someone's perspective on something, there's probably a blog out there about it. Some blogs start out small and personal. Then, through exposure, maintaining the blog can become a full-time job for some creators and earn them money through advertising. While private blogs do exist as a sort of high-tech journal, the main point of a blog is that it is a free platform where you can share something with an audience.

The following extract is from a blog written by Marcell Shehwaro, an activist describing the realities of life in 2014 in Syria during the internal armed conflict between opposing forces. The extract is from a post titled 'Syria: I Am Aleppo, Aleppo Is Me', published on the blog *Global Voices* on 12 March 2014.

> Living alone as an activist during wartime, alone and away from family and familiar surroundings, posed new challenges.
>
> …
>
> As one of the very few unveiled women in conservative and humble surroundings, among people who are very kind, despite the violence of their environment, I sometimes suffer from petrifying loneliness. I live with the constant fear of being kidnapped. At times I can withstand it, but at others I break down in exhaustion.

I am surrounded by stories of heroes whose heroism might inspire others to effect change themselves. Because of all this, and because our daily lives are full of events which may not be enough for one lifetime, I have decided to write for you. My articles will sometimes be about my everyday life. At other times they'll touch upon memories and what we would love our lives to be like, despite the horrors we see.

You are free to choose to sympathise with me, or be harsh with your judgements. But my hope is that what I relate to you reflects some of the dream, the desire to change, and the trust that this change is possible, as far-fetched or painful as that dream might be.

5.9 Check for understanding

1 Where is the city of Aleppo? Locate it on a map and record three facts about it below.

____

____

____

2 Marcell Shehwaro writes 'I have decided to write for you'. Who do you think she means by 'you'?

____

____

____

3 What do you notice about the length of sentences used by Marcell Shehwaro, and what is the effect of their length?

____

____

____

4 Circle the words below that describe the tone created in Marcell Shehwaro's blog

lighthearted hopeful reflective humorous

serious angry cheerful

5.10 Reflecting and discussing

Discuss the following questions in pairs, in small groups or with the whole class, as directed by your teacher.

1. What are some of the similarities between Alicia Bates' autobiographical writing, Anne Frank's diary and Marcell Shehwaro's blog?
2. Why might some people write a blog but keep it completely private?
3. Do you think a password-protected website is a safer place to keep personal writing than a physical diary?

Sentence structures

Various **language features** can enhance writing, including sentence patterns and clause structures. A **clause** is a grammatical unit that contains a **subject** and **verb**. The basis of a complete sentence is at least one clause. Writers sometimes embed additional clauses within a sentence in order to expand on the idea that the sentence introduces or to add extra information to the sentence. Look at the example below, taken from Marcell Shehwaro's blog post.

> Living alone as an activist during wartime, alone and away from family and familiar surroundings, posed new challenges.

The highlighted embedded clause adds helpful extra information and expands on the idea presented in the rest of the sentence: that being an activist and living alone during a war is challenging.

language features Features that support meaning (e.g. clause- and word-level grammar, vocabulary, figurative language, punctuation, images). Choices vary for the purpose, subject matter, audience and mode or medium
clause A grammatical unit referring to a happening or state e.g. 'the team won' (happening), 'the dog is red' (state), usually containing a subject and a verb group/phrase
subject A word or group of words (usually a noun group/phrase) in a sentence or clause representing the person, thing or idea doing the action that follows (e.g. 'The dog [subject] was barking')
verb A word class that expresses processes that include doing, feeling, thinking, saying and relating

5.11 Check for understanding

1. Write the above sentence from the blog without its embedded clause. Note that the sentence still makes sense.

____

2. What new information does the embedded clause give us about Marcell Shehwaro's situation?

____

The dystopian genre – frightening futures

A 'dystopia' is a controlling, corrupt or dangerous society. Dystopian fiction refers to stories that are set in such societies. These societies often develop following a war or environmental catastrophe, or when a society feels so frightened that it is willing to give up personal freedoms in order to feel safe again. Dystopian societies are totalitarian, which means they have a system of government that does not allow people to hold different opinions or views from those of the people or person in power. Sometimes, the effects of a dystopian society are hidden. Because the society might seem perfect, people might not even be aware that they are being controlled. This is where the hero often steps in: a character who discovers the truth about society and its rulers, and leads others to see that truth.

In this unit you will learn:

- about the conventions of the dystopian fiction genre
- how language can create imagery and atmosphere
- how to write your own dystopian story.

Curriculum content

Australian Curriculum content description	Content code
Explain the ways that ideas and points of view may represent the values of individuals and groups in literary texts, drawn from historical, social and cultural contexts, by First Nations Australian, and wide-ranging Australian and world authors.	AC9E8LE01
Share opinions about the language features, literary devices and text structures that contribute to the styles of literary texts.	AC9E8LE02
Analyse how language features such as sentence patterns create tone, and literary devices such as imagery create meaning and effect.	AC9E8LE05
Create and edit literary texts that experiment with language features and literary devices for particular purposes and effects.	AC9E8LE06
Use comprehension strategies such as visualising, predicting, connecting, summarising, monitoring, questioning and inferring to interpret and evaluate ideas in texts.	AC9E8LY05

Dystopian fiction

Hive, by A. J. Betts, is set in a claustrophobic series of chambers or vaults. These structures are known to their residents as 'the world', as they know nothing beyond their confines. The society in *Hive* is ruled by the mysterious Judge and a group of elders known as 'elect'. The citizens are classed according to the jobs they are raised to perform. The **protagonist**, Hayley, is a beekeeper who looks after the hives of bees that pollinate the fruit and vegetable gardens that feed the citizens. In this scene, Hayley recalls a frightening childhood lesson taught by one of the 'enginers', those in charge of the machines that keep this habitat livable.

protagonist The main character in a text

'Which of you children can tell me what is behind this door?'

'It's the service house,' I said, then corrected myself. 'It was the service house before the lights inside failed. It was a house for servicing the whole world.'

…

'The lights went out, yes – but why?' It was hard to see the elect's expression in the almost-dark. 'Which of you knows what really happened to ruin the lights? What did the servicers do to cause it?'

My heart skipped a beat. The servicers caused it? I looked to the other children, each as wide-eyed as I was.

'Bradley.' Teacher Sarah. 'Please.'

'What do you teach them, if not this?' He rapped solidly at the door behind him. I could barely breathe.

'What happened in the service house,' the enginer elect told us, 'was fire.'

Fire, he said, unlike the one that burned in the oven of the kitchen house. Fire, he described, like a monster. Fire that grew and growled and split into many monsters with greedy arms and tongues that chased the servicers who'd lived there in the first days. There was chaos, he said, as they all tried to get out but couldn't, for all three of their way doors had melted shut, the levers liquefying in their hands.

'The doors sealed. The servicers were trapped. Fire gobbled every single one of them.'

Darryl was sobbing. Was this still a lesson? Or had it become a story? It sounded like a dreadful story, but weren't stories supposed to begin with 'once upon a time'?

I turned to Teacher Sarah for confirmation. She was slumped against the doorframe. I wanted her to tell us this was just a story, but she didn't. With a voice that didn't soothe, she only said, 'It was long, long ago. Long before me.'

The fire was true? This really was a lesson?

'You children need to know what happens when you're not good boys and girls,' the enginer elect chided, 'when you don't say your prayers or follow instructions or do your chores. It's what happens when people get complacent –'

'Enough,' Teacher Sarah cried. Her hands clapped swiftly, interrupting the enginer and breaking his spell.

6.1 Reflecting and discussing

Discuss the following questions in pairs, in small groups or with the whole class, as directed by your teacher.

1 Two popular dystopian novel series are *The Hunger Games* by Suzanne Collins and *The Maze Runner* by James Dashner. Have you read these or watched their film adaptations? What are they about?

2 Can you name any other dystopian novels or films? What features do they have in common?

Dystopian settings

Societies in dystopian texts are the opposite of utopian societies. A 'utopia' is an ideal, fair and free society. Dystopian stories are usually set in the future, but sometimes this is a future that may appear to have gone backwards in terms of progress.

The features of a dystopian society include the following:

6.2

Check for understanding

1 Look up the following words from the extract from *Hive* and write a definition for each in your own words.

a liquefying ______________________________

b confirmation ______________________________

c soothe ______________________________

d chided ______________________________

e complacent ______________________________

2 What effect does the story of the fire have on the children?

____

3 What kind of behaviour is the engineer elect trying to encourage in the children by telling them this story?

____

4 The engineer elect's admission that the servicers – adults in charge of fixing machinery – caused the failure of the service house shocks the children. What does this suggest about the control of information in this society?

____

____

5 What other suggestions are there that this might be a dystopian society?

____

____

Dystopian protagonists

Every dystopian text needs a hero! The hero is almost always an underdog, a member of the society that most people disregard. The protagonist, however, sees the truth about the oppression of their society and typically finds some way to undermine or even destroy those in power.

Hayley starts to suspect that there is more to 'the world' in the vault than its citizens have been led to believe. Her curiosity leads to several horrific discoveries, including how the bodies of citizens who have died are disposed of, how the population is carefully controlled, and, eventually, the secrets of the service house. She is drugged by the elect in an attempt to make her forget, before the Judge's son, Will, finally shares the truth with her.

simile A device comparing 2 things that are not alike. Similes use 'like', 'as' or 'than' to make the comparison (e.g. The cake was as light as air)

The service house wasn't where flax had been grown or where fabric had been made with fancy tools. This was a house, the son told me, where people once used screens and phones to communicate with the other world.

'You mean the other houses?'

'I mean the other world.' The son's eyes flicked briefly up to mine then he slid the book away and dragged a new one to him. 'There's another world. Out there.'

'What do you mean out there?'

'Not in. Out.' His hand gestured at a wall.

'But how –'

'I'll explain later.'

'Explain now.'

'Morning is coming; you said so. There isn't time.'

He continued to read his brow creasing, his finger speeding across the words. His lips made clipped, indistinct sounds.

Forgotten by him, I turned to look at the pink-lit walls.

Out there?

I sized up the breadth and height of this house. It was just like every other, with three perimeter walls and three joining ones. It was a hexagon. Our world made up of nine hexagonal houses. Everyone knew that. The commons was central with six houses around it and two above it. It was our world. How could I envision anything else?

My heart fluttered. Not in? Out there?

...

Within me the truth unfurled, opening as a flower. I breathed as if for the first time.

I looked at each of the six walls, seeing them – seeing everything – anew. Just because this world was all I'd ever known, it didn't mean it was all there ever was.

6.3

Check for understanding

1 How do you know Hayley is shocked by the truth that the vault isn't the whole world?

____

____

2 How does the **simile** of the flower help to describe Hayley's realisation that she has been lied to her whole life?

____

____

3 Why might it be dangerous for Hayley if the Judge finds out that she knows the truth about the outside world?

____

____

4 What qualities does the following short extract reveal about Hayley's character? Circle three terms below the extract that you would use to describe her.

> It wasn't faith that made me go. It was stronger than that. Stronger also than fear.
>
> It was my body that led me, while my mind shouted reasons to stay. It was my body urging me forwards, to follow, to know.

curious	cowardly	brave	ignorant
selfish	compliant	defiant	

imagery Visually descriptive or figurative language to represent things including objects, actions and ideas in ways that appeal to the senses of the reader or viewer
metaphor A type of figurative language used to describe a person or object through an implicit comparison to something with similar characteristics

Latin and Greek word origins

Many words in English come to us from the classical languages of Greek and Latin. Often these are scientific or technical terms, because scientists and philosophers continued to use these languages long after everyday people stopped speaking them. However, you might be surprised to know that some very common words also come to us from these ancient languages, such as butter, which comes from Greek words meaning 'cow cheese'!

Analysing imagery

Imagery refers to the use of descriptive language that appeals to our senses (sight, hearing, taste, touch and smell) to create vivid mental pictures or sensations in our minds. It helps us visualise and experience the ideas, people, places and events described in a text more vividly.

Authors can also develop imagery through their use of figurative language such as similes and **metaphors**, as well as by choosing words with particular connotations (suggested ideas or feelings).

In the extract below, Hayley describes her relationship with the bees that she cares for.

> But sometimes solitude was exactly what I craved, and in those times I was especially grateful for the bees and the tranquillity I would find within the cage surrounding the hive. I would set Penny to a task – repairing a frame or pruning the salvias – while I sat wordlessly inside. The honeybees' constant humming didn't bother me, nor did their furry crawling along the edges of the cage and over me. I let them. They didn't sting me, and I wasn't an anomaly.
>
> I liked that the bees never asked if I was well or happy or hungry or upset or afraid. I liked that they never expected anything of me or monitored my expressions when things were changing ...
>
> At least here with the bees, I didn't have to pretend. Bees cared for nothing but the collection of pollen and the safekeeping of their babies.

6.4

Check for understanding

1 Find definitions for the following words from the extract:

a tranquillity ______

b salvias ______

c anomaly ______

2 Which words in the passage have connotations of peace and calmness?

______

3 Identify examples of sensory details that help contribute to this atmosphere.

a sight: ______

b sound: ______

c touch: ______

4 What evidence is there that Hayley feels free from other people's expectations while in the hive?

______

______

5 Overall, how would you describe the effect of the imagery in this passage?

______

______

Dystopian themes

Dystopian fiction is often based on an extrapolation (a prediction about what might happen in the future based on existing information) from current issues. It can be read as a warning to present-day society about what might happen if we continue down a particular path.

theme The main idea, concept or message of a text

Some common **themes** explored in dystopian fiction include:

- the rise of technology
- the individual versus society
- resistance to dictatorships
- environmental disasters
- loss of personal freedoms
- social inequality
- knowledge versus ignorance

In *Rogue*, the sequel to *Hive*, Hayley discovers the truth about the underwater vault she believed was the whole world. It was established as a giant seed bank, intended to preserve the world's plants following an apocalyptic disaster in which an asteroid hit the Earth. This creates a moral conflict within Hayley, as she wonders whether the elders were right to protect the seeds and those who live in the vault from the perils of the outside world.

'Whole buildings crashed down and everyone died because of the air blasts and shock waves,' Kid exclaimed with enthusiasm. 'Then earthquakes wrecked cities hundreds of kilometres away. And then there were tsunamis –'

'Parts of Europe did suffer,' Gigi continued, calmly, 'but the rest of the world got off lightly, all things considered. The biggest blow for Australia was the lack of services: power, water, and the internet.'

'The what?' I whispered to Kid, but he shrugged.

'Losing the Internet was the worst of it,' Gigi went on, 'because it meant there was no access to money. Everyone was suddenly the same kind of poor. People raided stores for tinned food and water, and no-one knew when things would return to normal, if ever. The dust clouds were a problem, but people managed, in the short term. They got used to not seeing the sun.'

...

Gigi made a low humming sound in her throat, then she lifted her gaze to the leafy ceiling, as if that's where the memories were stored.

'By the time the dust clouds finally lifted, a third of the crops had died. Then, after the bees disappeared, another third went too. That's when I was born, at the very end of pumpkins, apples, oranges, leafy greens, almonds and coffee. Then, after the alfalfa and lupin went, so did the livestock that ate them. Cows and sheep. Chickens, and more. The herbivores first, then the carnivores. They fell like dominoes.

6.5

Check for understanding

1 What would life have been like for the survivors after the crops failed? What problems do you think this would have caused for society?

____

____

____

____

2 Do you think the Judge and the elect were right to keep the truth from those living in the vault? Explain your answer.

____

____

____

____

Values in texts

Dystopian novels can reveal the **values** that a society believes in, and which the author fears are being eroded. Values are the ideals or principles that we believe are important.

In *Rogue*, Hayley learns many things about the world after the asteroid strike.

» Terrorism, climate refugees and environmental disaster have created a fearful world.

» Tasmania has been allocated as a territory for climate refugees, whose own countries were destroyed by environmental disasters such as rising sea levels.

» Those who live there now are tracked by 'blood codes' which are attached to their DNA profiles. This has led to an illegal trade in 'clean' or untraceable blood.

» The privileged people on mainland Australia live in tightly controlled high-tech cities, protected from outsiders.

values Ideas and beliefs specific to individuals and groups

The following values might be seen as being endorsed by *Hive* and *Rogue*.

freedom community truth individuality

education and knowledge environmental conservation

thinking for yourself empathy for others autonomy

Some that might be considered to be critiqued by these two novels include:

social control technological advancement self-interest

Dystopia in real life

The plots in *Five* and *Rogue* are extrapolated from real-life issues that concern many people today. While climate change and terrorism are well-documented global issues, A. J. Betts explores other fears as well.

6.6 Check for understanding

Use the internet to find real-world examples of these issues.

Issue in *Five* and *Rogue*	Example of this happening in the real world
Climate refugees As some countries are at risk of being overwhelmed by environmental issues such as rising sea levels, their populations may be forced to relocate elsewhere.	
Surveillance Governments continue to find new ways to monitor their populations, saying this is essential to maintaining public order.	
Social inequality People with wealth have access to services and privileges that are out of reach for other people.	
Seed banks As habitat loss and climate change threaten certain species, seed banks are being established to preserve seeds for the future.	

6.7 Get creative

Write your own dystopian story, using the steps below to help you.

1. **Choose a dystopian setting.** Think about a future world that is bleak, oppressive or unsettling. Consider real-life issues like government control and environmental issues, or another issue that may concern society today. What might this look like in the future?
2. **Develop your protagonist.** Create a main character who will navigate the dystopian setting. Think about their age, background, strengths and weaknesses. What challenges will they face in this world?
3. **Establish the dystopian society.** Describe the key features of this dystopian society. Is there a totalitarian government? Are there strict rules? Is there advanced technology? How do these elements affect the lives of ordinary people?

4 **Identify the main conflict.** Determine the central conflict of your story. It could be the protagonist's struggle against the oppressive system, a personal mission, or a battle for freedom and equality.

5 **Develop supporting characters.** Introduce other characters who will aid or hinder the protagonist in their journey. These can be friends, family members, mentors or adversaries (enemies or 'antagonists').

6 **Create rising action.** Build up the story by including obstacles and challenges that the protagonist must overcome. Show the ways in which the dystopian society attempts to suppress or control the protagonist, and how the protagonist works to overcome these.

7 **Build to a climax.** Reach a point of maximum tension and excitement in your story. This is where the conflict between the protagonist and the dystopian society comes to a head.

8 **Resolve the conflict.** Show how the protagonist confronts the conflict and resolves it, for better or worse. Maybe they escape, or maybe they find a flaw in the system, or even lead others into a rebellion.

9 **Now read over your story.** Consider how it might be improved. For example, ask yourself the following questions.

   a Have I used effective **language features** to help build atmosphere in my story, creating a sense of the dystopian world and my protagonist's thrilling journey?

   b Have I successfully conveyed the themes and messages I wanted my reader to consider?

   c Have I provided a sense of closure for the protagonist's journey that leaves my reader with something to think about?

10 Remember to let your imagination run wild and have fun while writing your dystopian story. Don't be afraid to experiment with unique ideas and twists that make your story stand out. Good luck!

language features Features that support meaning (e.g. clause- and word-level grammar, vocabulary, figurative language, punctuation, images). Choices vary for the purpose, subject matter, audience and mode or medium

UNIT 7

Performance poetry

From the travelling bands of ancient times to the rap battles and poetry slams of today, poetry has a long and rich history as an oral tradition. Performance poetry is a way of sharing stories important to a culture, as well as expressing the poet's perspectives on the world around them. Some poetic devices work as mnemonic tricks to help a poet remember their work, creating rhythm and musicality, while others construct evocative images to add impact to the poet's message.

In this unit you will learn:

- the conventions of performance poetry
- how to analyse a poem
- how to write and perform your own performance poetry.

Curriculum content

Australian Curriculum content description	Content code
Understand how layers of meaning can be created when evaluating by using literary devices such as simile and metaphor.	AC9E8LA02
Analyse how language features such as sentence patterns create tone, and literary devices such as imagery create meaning and effect.	AC9E8LE05
Create and edit literary texts that experiment with language features and literary devices for particular purposes and effects.	AC9E8LE06
Use interaction skills for identified purposes and situations, including when supporting or challenging the stated or implied meanings of spoken texts in presentations or discussion.	AC9E8LY02
Plan, create, rehearse and deliver spoken and multimodal presentations for audiences and purposes, selecting language features, literary devices, visual features and features of voice to suit formal or informal situations, and organising and developing ideas in texts in ways that may be imaginative, reflective, informative, persuasive and/or analytical.	AC9E8LY07

Performance poetry

Performance poetry, also known as 'spoken word' or 'slam' poetry, is a form of poetry that is intended to be performed before an **audience**. It offers dramatic presentation of the poem, with a strong emphasis on the poet's spoken word, vocal expression, gestures and body language to convey the meaning and emotion of the poem.

audience An intended or assumed group of readers, listeners or viewers that a writer, designer, filmmaker or speaker is addressing

Slam poets are known for tackling important social issues and deeply personal experiences. Their poems are creative and powerful expressions of their viewpoints on matters that are important to them. Through their performance, they aim to emotionally connect with their listeners. Many people find that seeing and hearing performance poetry is much more impactful than reading a poem in a book.

Jesse Oliver is a champion Australian performance poet. Originally from Perth, he is based in Melbourne where he continues to participate in poetry slams. Read one of Jesse Oliver's poems below.

Wake Up

My friends, wake up.

I know that in your dreams you see the way the
world should be, but we breathe.

In reality, your sleep,

it won't stay peaceful, even through a whisper of
evil, and there is evil in the minds of sleeping people
– wake up!

It's slipping through our fingers, the ability for
civility because clenched fists don't know what
they're fighting for. It's not love – wake up!

There you go.

Now rub that sleep from your eyes.

Arise and reply to those cries. Tell them why we despise the lies of a hateful enterprise.

Tell them that dream where nobody dies, and no one gets hurt,

and no one feels the emotional pain of being told that they are not the same.

Tell them we share 99.9% of our DNA so we don't know them by difference, we know them by name, or friend, and I would face my fears for the friends that I love because love is an infinite blanket.

I will pick apart the positive pieces of my past so that I can remember to thank it,

cos every single little bit of whittled brittle love in life could turn the world into a banquet

but this is not for the weak.

It's easy to sleep.

This takes strength because the heart is just a muscle and humans, we make mistakes but it's time to heal.

Too long have we reacted to the things that we feel and it's not true to who's inside us because we've all had bad thoughts,

but they don't have to define us.

It's time to trust that difference is not a threat to us no matter what it takes because food for hate is what fear makes, but you, you are awake.

So let's make a loud alarm clock on the dawn of this new day, a harm block for the new way with arms locked, standing strong

7.1 Reflecting and discussing

Discuss the following questions in pairs, in small groups or with the whole class, as directed by your teacher.

1. What was your initial response to the poem? What did it make you feel or think about?
2. What makes this poem powerful to you?
3. Have different people read the poem aloud. Does your experience of the poem change according to the ways different people perform it?

Figurative language

'Figurative language' refers to the use of words or expressions in a way that goes beyond their literal or dictionary meanings. It involves the use of figures of speech and literary devices to add depth, emotion, vivid imagery and layers of meaning to a poem.

7.2 Check for understanding

1 Draw lines to match the following figurative language devices with their examples.

simile	The dove represents peace and harmony.
metaphor	The flowers danced in the gentle breeze.
personification	The warm, yeasty scent of freshly baked bread wafted from the oven.
symbolism	Her smile was as bright as the sun.
sensory imagery	He's a shining star on the basketball court.

2 Write a definition in your own words for each of the figurative language devices.

a simile ______

b metaphor ______

c personification ______

d symbolism ______

e sensory imagery ______

3 Identify the devices used in the following quotes from 'Wake Up'..

a 'love is an infinite blanket' ______

b 'a whisper of evil' ______

c 'whittled brittle love' ______

d 'turn the world into a banquet' ______

e 'the dawn of this new day' ______

f 'love is our weapon' ______

g 'food for hate is what fear makes' ______

4 What do you think Jesse Oliver wants his audience to 'wake up' from?

____

____

5 Why is it 'easy to sleep'?

____

____

6 **Tone** refers to the speaker's attitude towards their subject matter, as expressed through their language choices. How would you describe the tone of this poem? Circle the three best answers below.

joyful	sarcastic	pleading	angry	sombre
frustrated	hopeful	defiant	sad	defeated

7 What does Jesse Oliver mean when he asks his audience to 'make a loud alarm clock'?

____

____

8 What social issue do you think this poem is exploring? Circle the answer below.

pollution   prejudice   homelessness

crime   poverty

9 What do you think the main idea of the poem is?

____

____

10 Write a paragraph analysing how three poetic devices are used to communicate this idea.

Hints for an effective paragraph:

- Use the TEEL (topic, evidence, explanation, link) formula to structure your paragraph.
- Use your topic sentence to state the main idea and the poetic devices used.
- In the next few sentences, explain how each poetic device contributes to the idea.
- Use quotes to support your explanations.
- In your linking sentence, reiterate the idea using different words.

tone The mood created by the language features used by an author and the way the text makes the reader feel

Tips for performing poetry

Go online and watch Jesse Oliver perform his poem.

Performing a poem in front of an audience may seem daunting; but with practice and attention to the following tips, you'll soon be performing like a true slam poet!

Understand the poem first:
Take the time to comprehend the meaning of the poem. Consider the themes, emotions and messages conveyed by the poet.

Practise pronunciation and diction:
Articulate each line clearly, checking on the pronunciation of challenging words.

Use appropriate expression:
Use appropriate tone and expression to capture the mood of your poem. Remember that this might change throughout the poem.

Develop pace and rhythm: Pay attention to the rhythm and flow of the poem. Vary your pace to suit the poem's structure, using pauses to highlight important moments or to create suspense.

Experiment with your delivery:
Experiment with variations in pitch, volume and pace to bring the poem to life.

Maintain eye contact and projection:
Maintain eye contact with the audience to engage them and project your voice confidently.

Use props or visual aids:
Consider props or costumes that complement the poem's content or theme. Make sure they enhance the performance rather than distract from it.

Rehearse and seek feedback:
Practise your performance to build confidence and familiarity with the poem. Seek feedback from teachers, peers or family members to improve.

Embrace stage presence:
Be aware of your posture and body language. Stand tall, use appropriate gestures and occupy the stage confidently.

Reflect the meaning: Aim to convey the poem's meaning to the audience through your performance. Show your understanding of the emotions and messages in the poem.

theme The main idea, concept or message of a text

7.3 Reflecting and discussing

Discuss the following questions in pairs, in small groups or with the whole class as directed by your teacher.

1. How different was Jesse Oliver's performance from that of the people in your class who read the poem aloud?
2. You can find clips on YouTube of other artists performing Jesse's poem, as well as several of Jesse's own performances. Watch a selection of these.
   a. Which performance did you find most impactful?
   b. What did you enjoy or find effective about this performance?
3. Try reading Jesse's poem aloud, experimenting with expression and pacing. How does this change the tone or emotion of the poem?

Bush ballads

Australian bush ballads are a unique and fascinating tradition in Australian literature. They use lively language and rhythms to capture the adventures and hardships of life in the Australian landscape. Bush ballads are like windows into a part of Australia's history, showing us the challenges and resilience of some of the people in our past. They are an important part of our country's heritage.

narrative The selection and sequencing of events or experiences, real or imagined, to tell a story to entertain, engage, inform and extend imagination, typically using an orientation, complication and resolution

Bush ballads are **narrative** poems; that is, they tell a story. They are characterised by regular line lengths, as well as strong patterns of rhyme and rhythm.

AB 'Banjo' Paterson was born in 1864 and grew up on a station known as Buckenbah, in western New South Wales. He was a bush poet, journalist and author, and has left a legacy of both humorous and serious poems about life in the bush. 'A Bush Christening' was first published in 1893.

A Bush Christening

On the outer Barcoo where the churches are few,
And men of religion are scanty,
On a road never cross'd 'cept by folk that are lost,
One Michael Magee had a shanty.
Now this Mike was the dad of a ten year old lad,
Plump, healthy, and stoutly conditioned;
He was strong as the best, but poor Mike had no rest
For the youngster had never been christened.
And his wife used to cry, 'If the darlin' should die

Saint Peter would not recognise him.'
But by luck he survived till a preacher arrived,
Who agreed straightaway to baptise him.
Now the artful young rogue, while they held their collogue,
With his ear to the keyhole was listenin',
And he muttered in fright, while his features turned white,
'What the divil and all is this christenin'?'
He was none of your dolts, he had seen them brand colts,
And it seemed to his small understanding,
If the man in the frock made him one of the flock,
It must mean something very like branding.
So away with a rush he set off for the bush,
While the tears in his eyelids they glistened –
''Tis outrageous,' says he, 'to brand youngsters like me,
I'll be dashed if I'll stop to be christened!'
Like a young native dog he ran into a log,
And his father with language uncivil,
Never heeding the 'praste' cried aloud in his haste,
'Come out and be christened, you divil!'
But he lay there as snug as a bug in a rug,
And his parents in vain might reprove him,
Till his reverence spoke (he was fond of a joke)
'I've a notion,' says he, 'that'll move him.'
'Poke a stick up the log, give the spalpeen a prog;
Poke him aisy — don't hurt him or maim him,
'Tis not long that he'll stand, I've the water at hand,
As he rushes out this end I'll name him.
'Here he comes, and for shame! ye've forgotten the name –
Is it Patsy or Michael or Dinnis?'
Here the youngster ran out, and the priest gave a shout –
'Take your chance, anyhow, wid 'Maginnis'!'
As the howling young cub ran away to the scrub
Where he knew that pursuit would be risky,

The priest, as he fled flung a flask at his head
That was labelled 'MAGINNIS'S WHISKY'!
And Maginnis Magee has been made a J. P.,
And the one thing he hates more than sin is
To be asked by the folk, who have heard of the joke,
How he came to be christened 'Maginnis'!

74

Check for understanding

1 What does it mean to be christened? What is involved in this rite?

2 Why is the boy afraid of being christened?

3 Banjo Paterson sometimes used non-standard spellings, such as 'divil'. Find three more examples in the poem and explain the effect that this technique creates.

4 This poem is said to celebrate Australia's 'larrikin' spirit.

a What does 'larrikin' mean? Circle the word from each pair below that best describes the qualities of a larrikin.

irreverent / respectful
humorous / serious
rough / refined
boisterous / quiet
well-behaved / mischievous
mean / good-hearted

b Do you agree with the statement that the poem celebrates Australia's larrikin spirit? Explain your answer.

____

____

5 What does life in the bush for the early settlers seem like according to this poem?

____

____

____

6 A stanza refers to a distinct group of lines in a poem. They usually function like paragraphs in a story. 'A Bush Christening' is written in quatrains; that is, four-line stanzas. Use the internet to find out the names of the following stanza lengths.

a two lines ______________________________

b three lines ______________________________

c five lines ______________________________

d six lines ______________________________

e seven lines ______________________________

f eight lines ______________________________

Sound devices

Bush ballads make use of a range of sound devices, such as rhyme, **alliteration** and rhythm. These function as mnemonic devices, which means that as well as making these poems sound interesting, they assist the speaker in memorising the poem. This tradition stems from poetry's origins as a form of oral storytelling, when bards would entertain listeners with long narrative poems known as 'epics'.

alliteration A recurrence of the same consonant sounds at the beginning of words in close succession (e.g. 'ripe, red raspberry')

7.5

Check for understanding

1 Add sound devices from the following list to the table below, matching them with their definitions.

end rhyme		internal rhyme	onomatopoeia
alliteration		assonance	consonance
sibilance	elision	rhythm	cacophony

Sound device	Definition
	a poetic device in which words imitate the sounds they represent
	a type of alliteration that specifically refers to the repetition of the 's' sound in nearby words
	the repetition of similar vowel sounds in nearby words, usually within a line or stanza
	the occurrence of rhyming words within a single line of poetry
	the repetition of consonant sounds in nearby words, usually within a line or stanza
	the repetition of similar sounds at the end of lines in a poem
	the repetition of the same consonant sound at the beginning of multiple words in a line or lines of poetry
	the pattern of stressed and unstressed syllables in a poem, to create the pace and flow of the poem
	the omission or contraction of a syllable or sound in a word or phrase to maintain the metre or rhythm of a poem
	the use of harsh sounds that create an unsettling effect (the opposite is euphony, where harmonious sounds create a pleasant effect)

2 Highlight the words that rhyme in each stanza of 'A Bush Christening', using different colours to represent the different rhyming sounds. What patterns can you see?

____

____

3 Write down an example of:

a end rhyme ________________________________

b internal rhyme ______

4 At times, Banjo Paterson tweaks the spelling of words to 'force' them to rhyme. Do you think this is a problem in this type of humorous poem?

______

5 Find examples of the following poetic devices in the poem.

a elision ______

b alliteration ______

c onomatopoeia ______

d simile ______

Rhythm and metre

Rhythm refers to the overall flow and musicality of a poem. Metre, on the other hand, refers to specific patterns of stressed and unstressed syllables that create particular rhythmical effects. The four most common types of rhythm are explained in the following table. Each individual part of the pattern is known as a 'foot'. Metre is usually defined also by how many feet are in each line, so iambic pentameter, the metre Shakespeare uses in his plays, has five iambic feet.

Iambic	Trochaic	Anapaestic	Dactylic
Each foot (an iamb) contains an unstressed syllable followed by a stressed syllable; e.g. 'com-PARE'.	Each foot (a trochee) contains a stressed syllable followed by an unstressed syllable; e.g. 'TROU-ble'.	Each foot (an anapaest) contains three syllables, the first two unstressed and the final one stressed; e.g. 'un-der-STAND'.	Each foot (a dactyl) contains three syllables, the first one stressed followed by two unstressed syllables; e.g. 'EL-e-phant'.
Shall *I compare* thee *to* a *summer's day*?	*Once upon* a *mid*night *dreary*	'Twas the *night* before *Christ*mas	*This* is the *for*est primeval

Three other features that contribute to the rhythm of a poem are to do with line structure:

» end-stopped: when a line of poetry concludes at the end of a sentence

» enjambment: when the sentence continues over subsequent lines

» caesura: a pause or break in the regular metre of a poem.

7.6 Check for understanding

1 Are the lines in 'A Bush Christening' mostly end-stopped or enjambed? Circle the correct answer.

end-stopped enjambed

2 How does this choice contribute to the pace of the poem?

____

____

3 The following lines have been split into separate syllables. Read them aloud, exaggerating where the emphasis naturally falls as you pronounce each word.

a Put a stroke (/) above each stressed syllable and a small cross (x) above each unstressed syllable.

On the out er Bar coo where the chur ches are few,

And men of re lig ion are scan ty,

On a road ne ver cross'd 'cept by folk that are lost,

One Mi chael Ma gee had a shan ty.

b What rhymical pattern or metre do you notice? Circle the correct answer below.

iambic trochaic anapaestic dactylic

c How many feet are in the first and third lines?

____

d How many feet are in the second and fourth lines?

____

e Why does Banjo Paterson elide (leave out) the first syllable of 'except'?

____

4 Take turns reading alternating stanzas aloud with a partner, trying to maintain this rhythm. Explain the effect it creates for the listener.

____

____

7.7 Get creative

Taylor Mali, an American author and poet, wrote a funny poem highlighting the need for careful editing of your work. It is called 'The the Impotence of Proofreading'. Here is the opening stanza.

> Has this ever happened to you?
>
> You work very horde on a paper for English clash
>
> And then get a very glow raid (like a D or even a D=)
>
> and all because you are the word1s liverwurst spoiler.
>
> Proofreading your peppers is a matter of the the utmost impotence.

Writing a great poem takes time. Poets will write several drafts, experimenting with word choice, **imagery** and rhythm until the poem feels right.

imagery Visually descriptive or figurative language to represent things including objects, actions and ideas in ways that appeal to the senses of the reader or viewer

Create a performance poem

phrase A group of words often beginning with a preposition but without a subject and verb combination (e.g. 'on the river'; 'with brown eyes'

Choose a topic: select a subject that you feel passionate about. It could be a personal experience, a social issue or anything else that inspires you.

Brainstorm ideas: brainstorm ideas related to your chosen topic. Write down words, **phrases** and images that come to mind. Don't worry about making them perfect at this stage.

Freewriting: set a timer for 5–10 minutes and start writing freely about your topic. Let your thoughts flow naturally and explore different ideas or emotions connected to your topic.

Create a structure: consider using stanzas to organise your ideas. Decide whether you want to have a specific rhyme scheme or metre or you prefer a free verse style.

Use figurative language: incorporate figurative language devices such as **similes**, metaphors and personification to make your poem more vivid and engaging.

Build imagery: engage the senses of your readers by including descriptive details that appeal to sight, sound, taste, touch, and smell.

Read aloud and revise: read your poem aloud. Pay attention to the flow, rhythm and sounds of your poem. Revise and **edit** your poem to make it more polished and impactful.

Add performance elements: consider how you can enhance your poem's delivery through your tone, pace, expression and body language.

Practise, practise, practise: rehearse your performance poem multiple times. Practise in front of a mirror or share your poem with friends or family members. Pay attention to your voice projection, articulation and stage presence.

Perform with confidence: when you're ready, get ready to perform your poem. Embrace the stage and share your unique voice and viewpoint with your audience.

Remember, the most important thing is to have fun and express yourself authentically through your performance poem. Let your creativity flow, and don't be afraid to take risks and experiment with different techniques.

simile A device comparing 2 things that are not alike. Similes use 'like', 'as' or 'than' to make the comparison (e.g. The cake was as light as air)

edit To prepare, alter, adapt or refine with attention to grammar, spelling, punctuation and vocabulary

Host a poetry slam

A poetry slam is when a group of poets meet to perform their work in a form of competition. They have three minutes to perform their poems, which are judged by the audience or a panel of judges. Each poet is scored on the content of their poem, their vocal delivery, their stage presence and the overall impact of the performed poem.

These are high energy events, but the poets are always respectful of each other's work. It is not always easy to step onto a stage and share something as personal as a poem. Competitors at slam events are known for cheering each other on and offering both praise and encouragement.

Design a score card like the one here. Decide on a panel of judges who will score each performance.

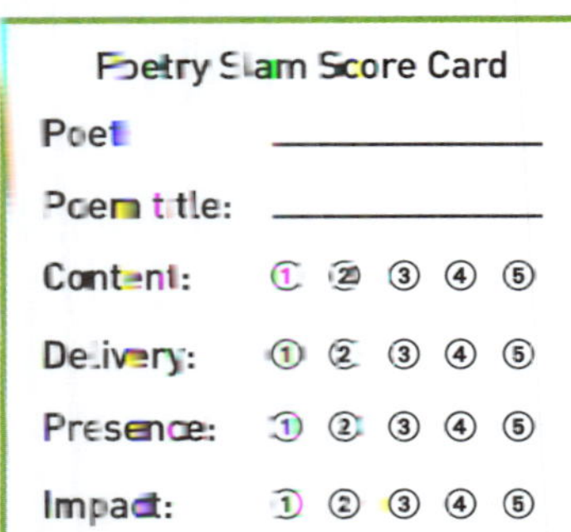

Poetry Slam Score Card

Poet: ____________

Poem title: ____________

Content: ① ② ③ ④ ⑤

Delivery: ① ② ③ ④ ⑤

Presence: ① ② ③ ④ ⑤

Impact: ① ② ③ ④ ⑤

After each performance, the judges should aim to give constructive feedback, identifying what they found effective within the performance as well as a target for future growth.

Australian film study: *Red Dog: True Blue*

Red Dog: True Blue is a 2016 Australian feature film directed by Kriv Stenders. It is a prequel to the 2011 film *Red Dog*, about a real-life kelpie called Red Dog that was well known for travelling throughout the Pilbara region of Western Australia. *Red Dog: True Blue* is an origin story, imagining a history for the iconic Red Dog and how he came to wander the lonely roads of the outback.

In this unit you will learn:

- how feature films communicate ideas and values
- how feature films can draw on other texts
- how camera angles and shots, as well as other multimodal language features, can shape the audience's response
- how to write an analytical paragraph using evidence.

Curriculum content

Australian Curriculum content description	Content code
Understand how cohesion in texts is improved by strengthening the internal structure of paragraphs with examples, quotations and substantiation of claims.	AC9E8LA04
Explain the ways that ideas and points of view may represent the values of individuals and groups in literary texts, drawn from historical, social and cultural contexts, by First Nations Australian, and wide-ranging Australian and world authors.	AC9E8LE01
Explain how language and/or images in texts position readers to respond and form viewpoints.	AC9E8LE03
Identify intertextual references in literary texts and explain how the references enable new understanding of the aesthetic quality of the text.	AC9E8LE04

Red Dog: True Blue

In imagining the life of Red Dog and the young boy who finds him as a pup, *Red Dog: True Blue* explores important **themes** of family, mateship and belonging. It also touches on some significant issues, such as mining and Aboriginal and Torres Strait Islander peoples connection to Country.

theme The main idea, concept or message of a text

8.1 Reflecting and discussing

Discuss the following questions in pairs, small groups or with the whole class as directed by your teacher.

1 Where is the Pilbara region? Look it up on a map. Has anyone in your class been there?

2 Where is the memorial statue of Red Dog located? Use the internet to find out. What does it suggest to you about how people felt about the real Red Dog that a statue was made of him?

3 Has anyone in the class seen the original *Red Dog*? What happens in this film? You might like to read some reviews of the film.

Understanding the exposition

The exposition refers to the beginning of a film, where the characters are introduced, the scene is set and future conflicts are hinted at. It is a very important part of any film, as it needs to engage the audience so they are invested in finding out how the film ends.

8.2 Check for understanding

Watch the first seventeen minutes of *Red Dog: True Blue*, then answer the following questions in the spaces provided.

1 Make a list of the characters who are introduced.

____

____

2 A montage is a series of short scenes or images, often put to music, that allows a filmmaker to quickly cover a time period. What does the montage used in the opening of the film suggest about Michael's adult life?

____

____

3 Use the internet to find the lyrics to the song played during the montage, 'Friday on my Mind' by The Easybeats. How does this song help you understand what Michael's life is like?

4 Why does Michael's son, Theo, desperately want a puppy?

5 List five reasons Michael gives for why getting a dog is 'a bad idea'.

6 When Michael and his sons are at the cinema, we get an over-the-shoulder shot which makes it look like Red Dog is looking straight at Michael, who starts to cry. Why do you think the director included this shot?

7 After taking his sons to see *Red Dog* at the cinema, Michael sits on Theo's bed and begins to tell him about Blue, his childhood dog. As he talks, the film flashes back to when Michael was a young boy, arriving in the Pilbara for the first time. What devices are used to help smooth the transition to a different time and place?

8 The opening scene is set in Perth. Compare this setting with the scene where Michael arrives in the Pilbara. Identify six differences in the colour and composition of these two settings.

9 Michael says that Blue was 'the first real mate I ever had'. How does this introduce the main theme of the film?

10 How does the young Michael feel about his first days at Warndurala Station? How does this change when he finds the puppy? What evidence do you notice that shows this change in emotion?

Themes

Themes are important ideas that are explored in a text, such as a film. They are developed through the characters and the conflicts that the characters experience.

The importance of mateship is a major theme in *Red Dog: True Blue*. Many of the characters who work at Warndurala Station live in relative isolation, undertaking sometimes dangerous work. Having a close companion or community is important in avoiding loneliness and staying positive. When Michael – nicknamed Mick – arrives at Warndurala to live with a grandfather he barely knows after having just lost his father, he finds it a lonely experience. Adopting Blue becomes an important way in which this internal conflict is resolved.

Some evidence for the theme of mateship includes:

» **Dialogue**: Mick says 'The fact was, it was lonely being in a new place without any friends. Seemed like everyone had a companion already.'

» **Visual language**: There is a montage of other characters and their companions, such as Big John play-fighting with Little John, and Durack receiving a plate of food from his wife.

8.3

Check for understanding

1 Complete the table below, adding two pieces of evidence to support each theme. For each theme, one piece of evidence should be a quote from the film's dialogue and the other should be an example of visual language.

Theme	Evidence: dialogue	Evidence: visual language
the importance of education		
respect for Aboriginal and Torres Strait Islander culture and traditions		
the challenges of growing up		
taking on responsibility		

2 Which of the five themes noted above do you think is the most significant in the film? Explain your answer.

____

____

____

Camera shots and angles

Camera angles	Examples	Shot types	Examples
A **high camera angle** shows characters and objects from above. It usually makes the viewer feel more powerful than the character.		An **extreme long shot** is used to set the scene and give an overview of a particular location or setting.	
A **low camera angle** shows characters and objects from below. It usually emphasises the importance or power of the character.		A **long shot** is often used to introduce characters to a scene or to provide more information about a setting.	

An **eye-level camera angle** shows a character or an object at the same level as the viewer's eyes. It is often used to express fairness or equality with the subject.

A **medium shot** is often used to show what a character is doing or capture them speaking.

A **bird's-eye camera angle** captures a scene or object by looking directly down from above it, as a flying bird would see things.

A **close-up shot** is often used to draw attention to facial expressions or particular objects.

A **point of view camera angle** captures a scene from the perspective of a character in the film.

An **extreme close-up** is often used to draw attention to very small details on objects or people.

8.4

Check for understanding

1. Find one still image from *Red Dog: True Blue* that represents each camera angle and distance. You could do this by taking a screen capture, finding images online or even taking a quick snap of the shot while the film is paused (the quality of the photo isn't important, as long as the scene is visible). Caption each with the type of shot, what it shows and what emotion or feeling it expresses.

For example: The high angle shot looking down on Blue makes the viewer feel that the puppy is helpless and in need of protection.

Audience responses

audience An intended or assumed group of readers, listeners or viewers that a writer, designer, filmmaker or speaker is addressing

The way a filmmaker crafts their images can have a big impact on how an **audience** responds. A 'response' refers to our reaction to the text: what we feel or think.

For example, when seeing the first image of the little puppy, covered in mud and trapped in an esky stuck in a tree following a cyclone, they may feel sympathy because of the puppy's small size, bedraggled appearance and vulnerability. As the **mise en scène** includes the aftermath of the cyclone, the audience may feel a desire to see Mick protect the puppy from further danger.

mise en scène In film, the composition of a shot, including elements such as lighting, costumes, props, set design and special effects

8.5

Check for understanding

1 Rewatch the scene where Mick trespasses in the cave, a sacred site for the local people (22:55–24:40). Tick which of the following aspects of the construction of this scene help to create a response of tension or anxiety in the audience.

a the darkness within the cave ☐

b the ominous music ☐

c the flickering torchlight ☐

d Blue's whining and barking ☐

e the close-up showing Mick's anxious face ☐

2 Add two more techniques from this scene used to create tension.

____

____

3 Identify scenes from the film that create the following responses in audiences.

a joy or amusement

____

b sadness or disappointment

____

c frustration or annoyance

____

4 For one of these scenes, explain how three techniques are used to generate the audience's response.

____

____

____

Issues and viewpoints

Red Dog: True Blue references some important issues within Australia. In the film, different characters have different viewpoints on these issues. A **viewpoint** is a particular belief or attitude that someone holds about a topic or issue.

For example, mining is a controversial issue, with different people having quite different viewpoints on it. Some people believe it is an important industry that supports families and the nation's economy, while others see it as an exploitation of Australia's resources, disrespectful to Aboriginal and Torres Strait Islander cultures, or as an environmental catastrophe. The film is set at a time when iron ore mining, a significant industry in the Pilbara region, was just beginning to take off. This is revealed in a scene in which Lang Hancock, a real-life mining magnate, visits Mick's grandfather at Warndurala Station, about 30 minutes into the film.

Look at the different viewpoints revealed in this scene in the following table.

Character	Viewpoint	Evidence
Lang Hancock	Mining is an important industry that will support people.	He taps out the red iron ore dust from Mick's comb and, pointing at it, says 'That is the future of this land, not that mob of wild short-horns in the bush out yonder.'
Grandpa	Mining is interfering with the rights of pastoralists (sheep and cattle farmers) like him.	When Mick asks whether the mining railway is a good thing, his grandfather replies 'No ... I can't stop it.' His stern voice, unhappy facial expression and folded arms reveal how angry he is with the impact on his livelihood.

In the same scene, another controversial issue is raised: that of who 'owns' the land on which Warndurala Station is located. The conversation between Lang, Mick and Grandpa reveals quite different viewpoints.

8.6

Check for understanding

1 Watch the scene from 30:40–32:30 and identify the four different viewpoints regarding land ownership that are expressed.

Character	Viewpoint	Evidence
Taylor Pete, a local Aboriginal man		
Grandpa, who runs the cattle station		
Mick, who has become friends with Taylor Pete		
the government, which takes back the land for a railway		

values Ideas and beliefs specific to individuals and groups

Values are qualities or ideals that we hold to be important. Typically, our viewpoints are shaped by what we value. For example, Mick's grandfather values the rights of the individual, which is why he is angry that the government wants to take some of his land for a railway, despite the fact that this will benefit many other people. He also values respect, hard work and responsibility, which he tries to instil in Mick.

2 Identify two values that you think influence each of the characters' viewpoints from Question 1.

a Taylor Pete: ______

b Mick: ______

c the government: ______

3 Match the following scenes with the values they promote. Choose from the following list of values. Use each value only once.

education perseverance loyalty justice

compassion respect for tradition responsibility

a Mick continues to try to learn how to ride the motorbike, despite his disastrous early efforts. ______

b Taylor Pete attends a rally about Aboriginal land rights. ______

c Mick decides to run away with Blue rather than be separated from him.

______

d Mick returns the stone he stole from the cave. ______

e Grandpa bends the rules to allow Blue to sleep in Mick's bedroom when he realises how lonely the boy is.______

f Grandpa tells Mick he has a duty to go back to his mother, despite his desire to stay at the station. ______

g Betty is employed to tutor Mick. ______

4 Identify three values that you hold, and explain why you feel them to be important.

______

______

______

Writing analytical paragraphs about a film

When analysing a film, as with any text, it is important that you include evidence to support your interpretation. This example paragraph illustrates how to incorporate both visual and auditory evidence to support your point.

The topic sentence introduces a clear point.

Dialogue is quoted using speech marks.

Specific film language terminology is used to describe the scene accurately.

The effect of the scene's construction on the audience is clearly explained.

The linking sentence reiterates the point made in the topic sentence.

Red Dog: True Blue explores the theme of mateship. Blue and Mick become constant companions, helping Mick to overcome his feelings of loneliness and not belonging in the outback. When Mick finds out he is being sent back to Melbourne without Blue, he tells his grandfather that 'Blue won't stay here without me', revealing the loyalty they share. The scene cuts to outdoors, where a high angle shot is used to look down on Mick and Blue and the station below them, gradually becoming an eye-level shot. The proximity of Mick and Blue shows their close relationship, while their distance from the homestead suggests their separation from the other characters on the station. Having the two figures in the foreground focuses the audience's attention on their relationship, while the mise en scène in the background reveals the isolation of their setting, reminding the audience of how lonely Mick would have been without Blue. Overall, this scene highlights the theme of mateship, and how important it is for people to have a companion in their lives to prevent loneliness.

Drawing on legends

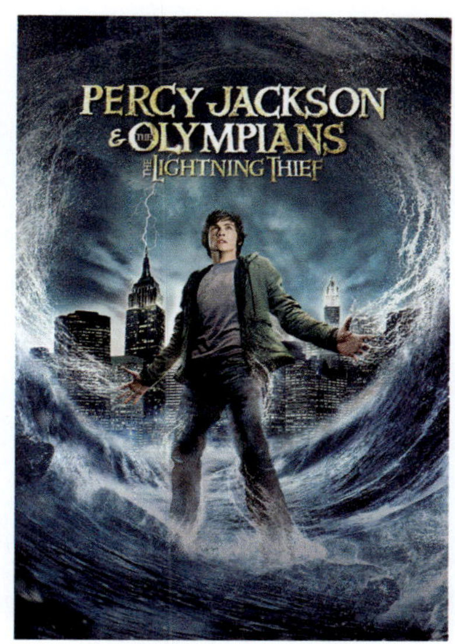

When the adult Michael takes his sons to the cinema, they watch *Red Dog*, a fictional film based on a real dog. Michael then reveals that the film was based on his childhood dog, Blue. *Red Dog: True Blue* unfolds as the prequel to *Red Dog*, flashing back to Michael's childhood when he adopted the puppy that was to become Red Dog.

Of course, this is all fiction, as no one really knows the origins of the real Red Dog. This complex interrelationship between the two films and the story of the real Red Dog demonstrates how writers and filmmakers can draw on myths, legends and even historical figures to create new and original stories.

Another example of this is *Percy Jackson & the Olympians: Lightning Thief*, a film based on the novel by Rick Riordan which takes figures from Ancient Greek mythology as inspiration for a new story set in today's world.

8.7 Reflecting and discussing

Discuss the following questions in pairs, in small groups or with the whole class as directed by your teacher.

1 What is the definition of a legend?
2 What does it mean when we call someone a 'legend' today?
3 Can you name any other films that draw on legendary figures? How many have you seen?
4 How have the filmmakers reimagined these stories to appeal to contemporary audiences? You might like to watch the trailers for some of these films to help answer this question.
5 Why do you think legendary figures remain a popular source of inspiration for filmmakers?
6 Using the internet, find out how many other books, films and other texts have been created from the legend of Red Dog.

8.3 Get creative

Think of a legend you would like to see adapted into a film. It might be a figure from mythology, a story from a cultural tradition, or a more contemporary legendary figure.

Imagine your class is a group of high-powered film executives. Write and deliver a two-minute pitch to convince them that the story you have chosen should be made into a film.

In your pitch, answer the following questions.

1 Why will the story translate well to the screen?
2 What themes are you hoping to communicate? What are you trying to say about the world and its people?
3 Where will it be set (time and place)? Will you keep to the traditional tale or will you adapt it for a modern **context**?
4 Where will you film it?
5 Who will you cast in the lead roles? Why will these actors suit the characters in the film?
6 Describe a key scene. How will you film it to create a strong impact on the audience?
7 Who will want to watch the film? How will this film appeal to their values?

Now go for the big sell: explain why people will flock to the cinema to see this film!

Remember: your aim is to convince them of the brilliance (and money-making potential) of your vision for the film. Be enthusiastic and inspiring in your delivery.

context An environment or situation (social, cultural or historical) in which a text is responded to or created. Or wording surrounding an unfamiliar word, which a reader or listener uses to understand its meaning

Feature film terminology

Complete the crossword to revise some of the language used in studying feature films.

Across

2. Speech between characters in a film.
6. Inanimate objects that an actor interacts with.
7. The specific and general locations where a film takes place.
9. Where one film scene ends and another begins.
11. How far the audience is from the focus of the action. Also known as shot size.
12. The direction that a camera points.
13. The direction, source, quality and colour of light used to create atmosphere in a film.

Down

1. The process of arranging film and sound recordings into a sequence.
3. The emotion communicated on an actor's face, along with their body language.
4. The images recorded continuously from the time the camera starts until the time it stops.
5. The clothing worn by a character.
8. A specific part of a film's narrative that captures a specific event, involving particular characters at a certain time and place.
10. Tunes used to accompany the action in a film.

UNIT 9

Dive into drama

The theatre is an exciting place where actors, along with sets, props, costumes, sound effects and lighting managed by a backstage crew, work together with the director to bring life to the stories imagined by the playwright. What is special about stage drama is that you get to see everything happening right in front of you, watching the story unfold in real time. Stage drama is a storytelling experience like no other.

In this unit you will learn:

- important theatre terminology and the conventions of script writing
- how to select language for specific characters and use punctuation effectively
- how to create a stage play script using elements of narrative.

Curriculum content

Australian Curriculum content description	Content code
Recognise how language shapes relationships and roles.	AC9E8LA01
Understand and use punctuation conventions including semicolons and dashes to extend ideas and support meaning.	AC9E8LA09
Plan, create, edit and publish written and multimodal texts, organising and expanding ideas, and selecting text structures, language features, literary devices and visual features for purposes and audiences in ways that may be imaginative, reflective, informative, persuasive and/or analytical.	AC9E8LY06

Stage drama

Stage drama is an exciting form of storytelling that is performed live in a theatre. **Audiences** are captivated by actors who bring characters to life. The words they speak, written by talented playwrights, move the story forward and explore important **themes**, conflicts and relationships.

audience An intended or assumed group of readers, listeners or viewers that a writer, designer, filmmaker or speaker is addressing
theme The main idea, concept or message of a text

9.1 Reflecting and discussing

Discuss the following questions in pairs, in small groups or with the whole class, as directed by your teacher.

1. Has anyone ever told you 'You're so dramatic?' What does this mean?
2. Have you ever been to see a play or a musical? What did you see? Was it more or less exciting than going to the cinema or reading a book?
3. Think of a film or a novel that you would love to see as a stage play. What would be the most exciting part?

Read the opening of the play 'Scrambled Eggs' by Sue Murray.

Characters

BELLA

HANNAH

CHELSEA

MISS RYAN – A teacher

MR OSMETTI – A teacher

MRS BENSON – Bella's mother

BRETT – Hannah's father

Setting

The school, a restaurant and various homes. Scene changes are established by the actions of the characters. A kitchen bench and some cooking equipment, a table, five chairs and small props are needed.

SCENE 1

MISS RYAN and MR OSMETTI enter. Miss Ryan is carrying a little box.

MR OSMETTI:	Another day, another dollar. And only thirty-nine more teaching days until Christmas.
MISS RYAN:	And counting, Mr Osmetti.
MR OSMETTI:	Frank. Call me Frank. [Pointing out the box] What's that?
MISS RYAN:	Oh, something for my life skills unit.
MR OSMETTI:	Another one of your pet projects, eh?
MISS RYAN:	[Nodding] Pet is right.
MR OSMETTI:	Okay, tell me.
MISS RYAN:	Well, it's a project to teach responsibility, to give the students a taste of what it's like to be a parent. I've challenged them to care for an egg for a weekend.
MR OSMETTI	An egg?
MISS RYAN:	Yes. And I've stamped each one so the students can't replace their egg in the case of an accident. And they have to keep a log book explaining what they've done over the weekend and how they cared for the egg.
MR OSMETTI:	Cared for it? Like feeding it and washing it?
MISS RYAN:	No. How they do their normal weekend activities while looking after the egg. If they can't watch it themselves, they have to arrange a babysitter.
MR OSMETTI:	Oh, sure. I can just see Mitchell Ferguson asking his father to babysit his egg.

9.2

Check for understanding

1 Label the parts of the script extract above using terms from the list below. If there are any terms you don't know, you can find their definitions over the next few pages

title	setting description	stage directions	dialogue
cast list	prop	scene title	

2 Explain the project that Miss Ryan has just given her students.

____

____

3 Does Mr Osmetti think that the project is a good idea? How do you know this?

____

____

4 Are Mitchell Ferguson and his father likely to take the project seriously? How do you know this?

____

____

5 From the list of words below, circle one word that you think best describes Mr Osmetti's attitude towards his job, and underline one word that you think best describes Miss Ryan's attitude towards her job.

enthusiastic	frustrated	eager	indifferent
doubtful	serious	irritated	optimistic

Theatre terminology

Acts and scenes

Most plays are written with a linear structure that incorporates an exposition, climax and resolution. Longer plays might stretch this over three or even five 'acts', which are broad sections of the play's plot. Shorter 'one-act' plays with less complicated plots do this in a single act. 'Scenes' are smaller parts within an act, capturing specific moments in the story.

Here is an overview of the way 'Scrambled Eggs' is structured.

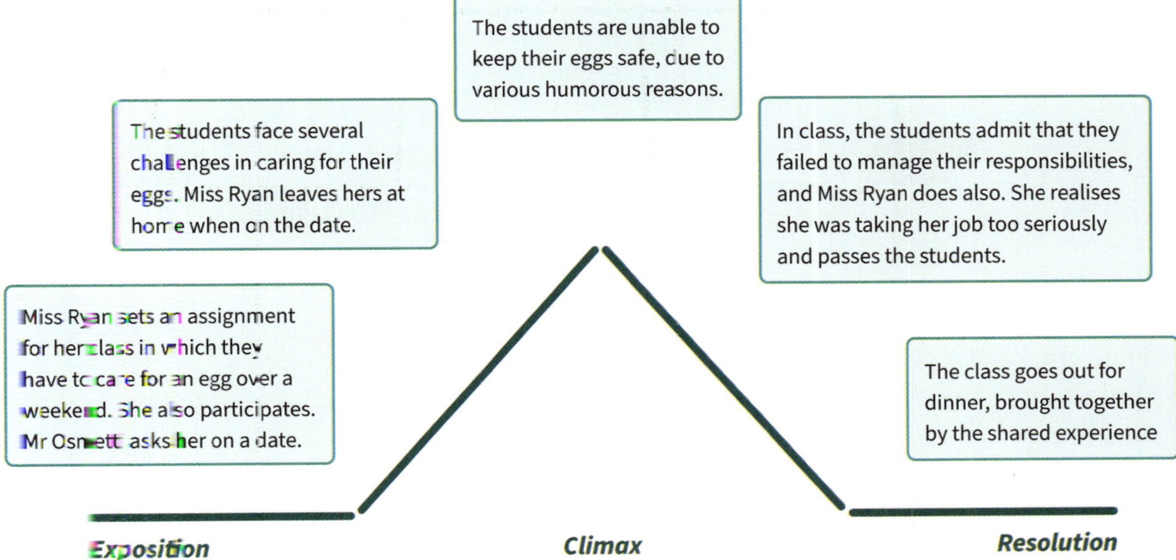

Stage directions

There are different types of stage directions included in a script. These are typically written in italics. They can be used to:

» outline the overall setting of the play. This is typically done at the beginning of the script.

» describe the set and props needed for each scene. These descriptions can include character placement or movement as the lights go up. They are found at the beginning of each scene.

» provide instructions to guide actors regarding movement, actions, body language and expression. These are typically enclosed in square brackets and are included with the dialogue.

Positions on stage

Stage directions often indicate where an actor should enter, exit, stand or move. These positions are illustrated below.

Speech terms

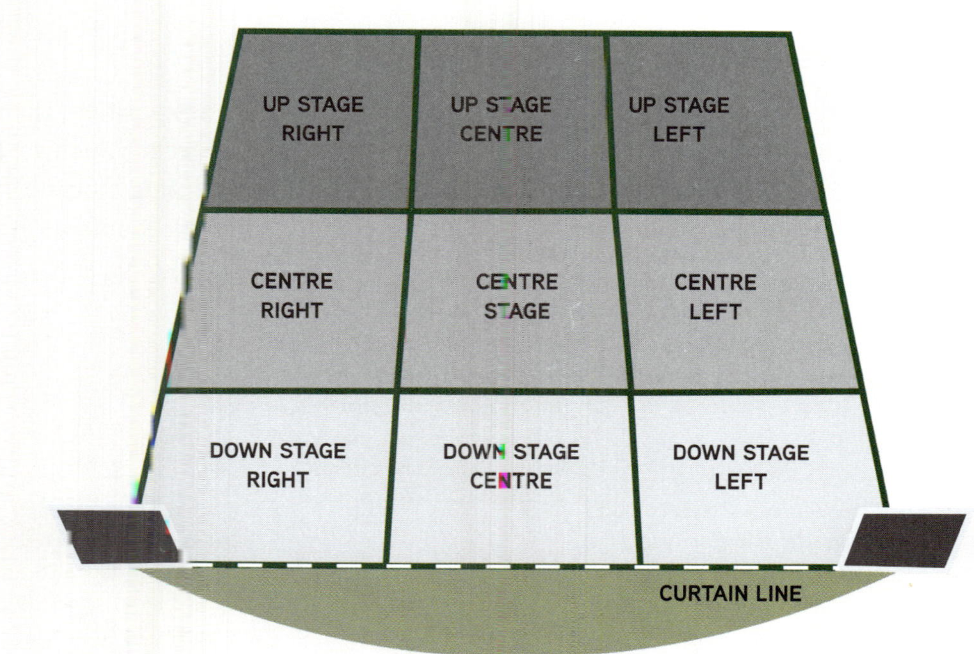

Most of a script is composed of dialogue – the speech that occurs between characters. It is a vital part of any play! Dialogue needs to keep the plot moving along, create interesting and recognisable characters, and entertain the audience.

Here are some particular types of speech found in plays.

Dialogue	Speech that occurs between two or more characters.
Monologue	An extended speech by one character, delivered to others on stage or directly to the audience.
Soliloquy	An extended speech by one character, given as if talking to themselves, providing an insight into their thoughts and feelings (the other characters aren't present or, if they are on stage, don't hear it).
Aside	When a character speaks directly to the audience without the other characters hearing.
Beat	A dramatic pause within the dialogue.

Staging elements

A playwright might include descriptions of how they would like the stage to look, but often it is the director who makes these decisions, interpreting the playwright's script in their own way. Aspects of staging include the following.

Scenery	Painted backdrops or 'flats' (upright panels), as well as furniture and other props that establish the setting of the play.
Props	Physical items that enhance the storytelling. They can range from everyday objects like books or furniture to objects that are used by characters, such as a sword or kitchen utensils.
Costumes	The clothing worn by a character, which gives audiences a visual clue about their personality or role in the play.
Lighting	The colour, intensity and nature of lighting used to help create atmosphere and indicate changes in a scene.
Sound effects	Music and other sounds that assist in the storytelling, such as a door slamming, a gunshot or thunder.

9.3 Check for understanding

1 Describe the following parts of the set design in the picture.

a scenery: ______________________

b props: ______________________

c lighting: ______________________

2 What costumes would you use to show the personalities of the following characters?

a Miss Ryan: ______________________

b Mr Osmetti: ______________________

Script writing conventions

There are particular rules or **conventions** that all scripts follow. These make it easy for directors and actors to read a script, and for the cast and crew to quickly identify the playwright's intentions for how characters should act, as well the instructions about staging, costumes and props needed.

Here are the conventions that you will find in a typical drama script.

1 Title: all plays need an engaging title.

2 Character list: a list of all characters in the play is provided at the beginning, sometimes with a very brief description of their roles or relationships to other characters.

3 Setting description: the setting that appears at the beginning of the play is described in detail (this also happens at the beginning of each of the acts if the setting changes).

4 Scene description: these descriptions appear at the beginning of each scene and describe how the scene is to begin. They are written in present **tense** and are typically in italics.

5 Stage directions: these square-bracketed instructions are used to indicate:

- how certain lines are to be spoken, such as [timidly], [shouting] or [tearfully]
- character entrances and exits
- sound or lighting effects

» character movement and action, such as [banging his fist on the table], [shaking her head] or [crosses to stage left].

6 Dialogue: apart from stage directions, scripts consist largely of speech between characters. The character's name is usually written in capital letters and separated from dialogue with a **colon**.

7 Punctuation: a range of punctuation is used to indicate pausing, pacing and expression. Capital letters, ellipses, dashes, commas, exclamation marks, question marks and full stops provide actors with suggestions about how to deliver their lines.

convention An accepted practice that has developed over time and is generally used and understood (e.g. use of punctuation)
tense The form a verb takes to signal the location of a clause in time (e.g. present tense 'has' in 'Jo has a cat' locates the situation in the present; past tense 'had' in 'Jo had a cat' locates it in the past)
colon Punctuation mark (:) that separates a general statement from one or more statements that give extra information, explanation or illustration. Statements after a colon do not have to be full sentences

Using punctuation purposefully

You should be familiar with most types of punctuation that you will encounter in a script; however, you should familiarise yourself with the following rules.

» A dash (—) shows that the character has been cut off or interrupted. They did not get to finish their thought before another character started speaking or another action took place.

» An ellipsis (…) shows unfinished thoughts. It signifies a trailing off or a moment of hesitation.

» A colon (:) is typically used to indicate that a character's dialogue is about to begin. It is placed after the character's name and is followed by the spoken lines.

» All lines of dialogue should be finished with either a full stop (.), a question mark(?) or an exclamation mark (!), unless a dash or ellipsis is being used for effect.

» Square brackets ([ ]) are used to show stage directions such as expression or actions performed by the character. Text within the square brackets is not spoken.

edit To prepare, alter, adapt or refine with attention to grammar, spelling, punctuation and vocabulary

9.4 Check for understanding

1 The extract below has some incorrectly used or missing punctuation marks. **Edit** the passage, adding the correct punctuation.

SCOUT	Did you hear about the school dance next week
CHARLIE:	Yeah, I'm just not sure if
	Charlie turns around
SCOUT	Don't worry, there'll be worse dancers than you there

Staging, costumes and props

When producing a play, the first thing to do is explore the play script, reviewing the dialogue and stage directions. Secondly, it is important to consider all the visual elements that will be involved in bringing the story to life on stage, including:

Staging	Costumes	Props
Sets and backdrops, used to create a sense of the setting of the play. These range from realistic to containing just a few symbolic elements to suggest the setting	What the characters are wearing. Costumes are carefully chosen to suit the character, their personality, and their role within the play.	Items that are needed on stage. Some of these contribute to the setting but some of them are important objects used by the characters.

Sometimes these elements are indicated by the playwright, but often the director will make their own choices about staging.

Using stage directions

In the same way that we can select language carefully to construct dialogue for characters, playwrights use stage directions carefully to help reveal the plot. Read the example below.

Early morning, in a classroom. There is a broken computer on the floor next to the teacher's desk. MR PATEL enters and sees MATEO. Both seem shocked.

MR PATEL: [Shouts] What are you doing?!

MATEO: [Nervous] Nothing!

[Mateo steps away from the computer and looks down at his feet.]

9.5

Check for understanding

1 What part of the script above makes you think that Mr Patel has assumed Mateo has broken the computer?

___

2 What part of the script makes you think that Mateo actually is guilty?

___

3 Read the following script written without any stage directions.

OLIVIA:	Good morning, Miss Tran.
MISS TRAN:	Good morning, Olivia.
OLIVIA:	What are we doing today?
MISS TRAN:	First, I'm going to check your homework.
OLIVIA:	Great.
MISS TRAN:	Then we're going to take down some notes.
OLIVIA:	Awesome.

Select two lines from the dialogue above and rewrite them to suit the following scenarios, adding stage directions to indicate actions and how the dialogue is to be spoken.

a The two characters have a positive relationship and both are happy to talk to each other.

____

____

b Miss Tran likes Olivia and is trying to win her over but Olivia does not like Miss Tran.

____

____

c Olivia likes Miss Tran and is trying to win her over but Miss Tran does not like Olivia.

____

____

Developing unique voices for characters

Have you ever noticed that you can normally tell which of your friends or family members has spoken because you recognise their voice? This is not just because we remember the way they sound but also the way they speak.

Writing characters in a play is no different. They should not all sound the same. Instead, their personalities and mood should come through in the way they speak, both in terms of the language they use and how the stage directions indicate their words should be spoken.

Read the following extract from 'Scrambled Eggs'.

SCENE 15

A small table and two chairs are placed on stage. MISS RYAN and MR OSMETTI enter and sit at the table.

[BELLA and MRS BENSON enter. MRS BENSON is carrying the egg proudly.]

BELLA Mum, maybe we should just tuck the egg in your bag or something. People are looking.

MRS BENSON: You take it, Bella. It's your baby after all.

BELLA: No, no, really, Mum.

MRS BENSON: Go on. Oh, isn't that your teacher? Miss Ryan? And who is she with? Mr Confetti, or whatever his name is.

BELLA: Where? Oh, Mr Osmetti, Mum let's just sit …

MRS BENSON: [Waving at MISS RYAN] Yoo-hoo!

[MRS BENSON makes a beeline for MISS RYAN and MR OSMETTI, holding the egg basket aloft. BELLA trails behind.]

MRS BENSON: Miss Ryan, hello, I'm Bella's mother.

MISS RYAN: [Embarrassed] Oh yes, good evening. Hello Bella.

BELLA: Hello.

MRS BENSON: I wish school was such fun when I was a girl. And I can report that Bella is taking her assignment very seriously. [She holds up the basket.] We love our little Eggberta.

BELLA: Mum.

MRS BENSON: And I believe you're taking part too, Miss Ryan? Such commendable dedication. Such a good example.

MISS RYAN: Oh, yes, well umm …

MRS BENSON: And I guess you'll have to get home early, if you have a sitter waiting!

MISS RYAN: Oh, well, you see …

BELLA: Mum, come on. Let's find a table.

MRS BENSON: When I was at school, I thought teachers got put in the cupboard at night, like a vacuum cleaner.

MISS RYAN: But as you can see, we get time off for good behaviour.

MRS BENSON: Pardon?

BELLA: Mum – come on. Let's see if there's a table in the courtyard.

MRS BENSON: Enjoy your dinner, you two. Ciao. [BELLA and MRS BENSON exit.]

MR OSMETTI: What a motor mouth.

9.6

Check for understanding

1 Why is Miss Ryan embarrassed to be seen by Bella and Mrs Benson?

2 How do we know she is embarrassed?

3 Miss Ryan makes a joke about teachers getting time off for good behaviour and Mrs Benson replies with 'Pardon?' What is the most likely reason Mrs Benson asks Miss Ryan to repeat herself?

a She didn't hear her speak.

b She didn't realise she was making a joke.

c She was too busy making sure Eggberta was safe.

4 Below is a list of words that could describe the voices of characters. Sort the words into the table below to show which character's voice they best suit.

laid-back cheerful agitated stressed

humorous polite confident happy

uneasy worried proper old-fashioned

intense concerned

Mr Osmetti	Miss Ryan	Mrs Benson

Writing interesting conversations

When you write a script, it is important that you write dialogue that is authentic. This means that it sounds like a realistic conversation between your characters. However, it also needs to move at a pace appropriate for the situation, moving the plot along and keeping the audience engaged.

Imagine that your teacher asked you, 'How much of your assignment have you completed?' If you answered this question factually, you might say, 'I have done the first 300 words and I have 500 left to go.' But this is not normally how we respond. A more likely response may be one of the following.

- 'When is it due again?' This is answering a question with another question.
- 'How much have I done?' This is repeating the question back to the speaker.
- 'Oh, I had soccer training last night.' This is explaining the reason you have or haven't done something, without answering the question.

This can be an interesting way to build tension in your plot or between your characters.

9.7

Check for understanding

1 Write a short passage of dialogue between two characters. The characters and situation can be of your choosing. Select language carefully to show what your characters' personalities are like.

____

____

____

____

____

____

2 With a partner, read your dialogue aloud. Does it sound authentic for each character? Explain what you tried to communicate about each character through their dialogue.

____

____

____

Direct and indirect speech

You can use a mixture of direct and indirect speech to build tension. Direct speech in a drama script is when the words spoken by a character reflect their own thoughts. Indirect speech is when a character reports what another character has said without using their exact words, but still conveying the meaning or content. Often this is used to report on actions that have not been represented onstage.

Direct speech		Indirect speech	
MR KARLSEN:	You need to work much harder in Science if you are going to get an A grade this semester.	DAD:	[Putting down phone] Mr Karlsen says you aren't working hard enough in Science. What's the story?
XANDER:	I'm trying! I need some help with this chemistry topic. It's really hard.	XANDER:	I'm trying, Dad! I told Mr Karlsen I need more help but he's too busy.

9.3

Get creative

1 Read the following extract from Michael Gerard Bauer's 2006 novel *Don't Call Me Ishmael*. In this extract, Ishmael describes a terrible prank that his classmates played on his friend James Scobie.

> Looking back, I suppose I should have done something or warned him in some way, but what could I have said or done that would have made any difference? Everything *seemed* normal enough, and though I knew *something* was going to happen, I had no idea what it was or exactly where or when it would unfold. I did try to catch James Scobie's eye, but he just nodded once, sat down and started to unpack his bag. It wasn't until he placed both hands on the lid of his desk and began to lift that the memory of Danny Wallace sitting on top of it flashed into my mind and I finally knew at least where the danger lurked.
>
> But it was too late, James Scobie had already straightened his arms and pushed up the lid.
>
> A blur of wings exploded from within. It was like a scene from *The Mummy*, *Arachnophobia* and *A Bug's Life* all rolled into one. First about a dozen enormous green and brown grasshoppers catapulted themselves into the air smacking into windows, leaping past startled faces and clapping their sharp spiky legs into unsuspecting hair, necks and limbs. This led to random outbreaks of what appeared to be the Mexican hat dance around the class.
>
> Then three enormous stick insects the size of rulers roared into the air with humming, purple wings. Unfortunately, one immediately flew up into the fan and was slung across the room, hitting the white board with a sickening *Thwuug*! before sliding down slowly and messily to the ground.

> One landed with a thud on Bill Kingsley's back and held on for all it was worth until Bill Kingsley ripped his shirt off in panic and flung it unintentionally over Doug Savage's head. This in turn caused a strange rapidly escalating growl to rise from Doug Savage as he madly tore the shirt from his head and sent it sailing out the window and into the playground three storeys below. The third stick insect continued to sweep around the room like a Black Hawk helicopter while everyone ducked and dived for cover.

2 In your English notebook rewrite the above extract as a drama script. Remember to include the following:

- At the start of your scene, write stage directions that describe the setting.
- Write the name of each character who is speaking, followed by a colon.
- Use stage directions in brackets to show the lines are to be spoken, or to describe actions.
- Create additional dialogue to develop the characters within this scene. Use language that reflects their personalities.
- Use punctuation to indicate pausing, pacing and expression. Ellipses, dashes, commas, exclamation marks, question marks and full stops should be used when appropriate.

3 Once you have completed your draft, follow the steps below to proofread and edit your script.

a Read the script aloud to identify awkward phrasing and unclear instructions.

b Ensure consistency in character names, settings and stage directions.

c Evaluate dialogue for authenticity and character consistency.

d Clarify stage directions, ensuring clear and precise instructions.

e Check for grammar, punctuation and spelling errors.

f Seek feedback from others and revise accordingly.

g Polish the script and conduct a final check for mistakes.

h Practise reading and rehearsing with a group to find other ways to improve your script.

UNIT 10

Communicating clearly

Both at school and in your life outside of school, you will encounter many situations in which you will need to communicate information clearly and concisely. Learning to do so is an important skill. Whether in reports, infographics, presentations or even everyday conversations, sharing information in ways that are precise, credible and clearly structured will ensure that you are a top communicator!

In this unit you will learn:

- how to use precise vocabulary
- ways to reference quotes and other sources of information
- how to structure information texts such as reports and infographics.

Curriculum content

Australian Curriculum content description	Content code
Explain how texts are structured depending on their purpose and how language features vary, recognising that some texts are hybrids that combine different genres or elements of different genres.	AC9E8LA03
Identify and use vocabulary typical of academic texts.	AC9E8LA08
Analyse and evaluate the ways that language features vary according to the purpose and audience of the text, and the ways that sources and quotations are used in a text.	AC9E8LY03
Plan, create, edit and publish written and multimodal texts, organising and expanding ideas, and selecting text structures, language features, literary devices and visual features for purposes and audiences in ways that may be imaginative, reflective, informative, persuasive and/or analytical.	AC9E8LY06

Informational texts

Informational texts are written materials that provide factual information about a particular topic. They are designed to help readers gain knowledge and understanding about various subjects. Unlike fictional texts, informational texts are primarily focused on presenting facts, explaining concepts, and sharing information in a straightforward and clear manner.

These texts can cover a wide range of topics such as science, history, geography, current events, technology, culture and more.

10.1 Reflecting and discussing

Discuss the following questions in pairs, in small groups or with the whole class, as directed by your teacher.

1 Which of the following informational texts do you regularly use?

textbooks encyclopaedias websites

educational videos infographics newsletters brochures

infographics newsletters brochures pamphlets

reports minutes of meetings news reports

non-fiction texts reviews

What sorts of procedural texts have you followed?

2 Some texts combine information with persuasive or **evaluative language.** For example, reviews offer information about a product or service combined with the writer's opinions. Can you think of other examples of texts that blend information with evaluative or persuasive elements?

evaluative language Positive or negative language that judges the worth of something. It includes language to express feelings and opinions; make judgements; and assess quality of objects, ideas and features of texts

Informational reports

A report is a common type of informational text. You may have written reports yourself for subjects such as Science and Geography. Read the following example of a report and notice the features that have been annotated.

Scan the QR code or click **here** to access the report.

10.2

Check for understanding

1 Use a dictionary and write down definitions of the following technical terms from the report

a biodiversity ______________________

b ecosystem ______________________

c mosaic ______________________

d fire-prone ______________________

e stewardship ______________________

2 What is the main **purpose** of this report?

____

3 How do the subheadings help guide the reader through the report?

____

____

4 Why does the writer include a photograph?

____

5 Identify three **language features** that make the writer sound knowledgeable about the topic of the report.

__________________ __________________ __________________

purpose An intended or assumed reason for a type of text
language features Features that support meaning (e.g. clause`- and word-level grammar, vocabulary, figurative language, punctuation, images). Choices vary for the purpose, subject matter, audience and mode or medium

Language style in informational texts

Informational texts are characterised by an academic style, which means they aim to be objective and factual, communicating information in a clear, concise and credible manner. The language they use is an important factor in creating this academic style.

10.3 Check for understanding

Find definitions for the following stylistic features, as well as examples from the previous report. Some have been completed for you.

Stylistic feature	Definition	Example from the text
formal language		
technical terminology	specialised words or terms that are specific to a particular field or subject	
objective or neutral tone		This may be during cooler months, when there is less chance of a fire becoming out of control.
concise language		
subordinate clause	a clause that cannot stand as a complete sentence, used to add information, provide context, or establish relationships between ideas	
transitional words and phrases		*The Kiwirrkurra people also use mosaic burning …*
active tense	a grammatical structure in which the subject of the sentence performs the verb, used to convey direct and straightforward information	
quotes from experts		

Citing sources

Citing or referencing your sources of information is an important part of academic and research writing as it gives credit to the original authors and allows readers to find more information if needed. It is important to use trustworthy sources of information so that your research is accurate and credible. Here are some ways of citing sources.

1. In-text citations: when you quote a source within your writing, you need to include an in-text citation. This is done by mentioning the author's name and the year of publication in parentheses after the information you are citing:

   'According to Smith (2019), climate change is a pressing issue.'

2. Reference list: at the end of your work, include a reference list that provides full details of all the sources you used. A bibliography is similar, but includes all the sources you researched, and not just those you cited. The reference list should be organised alphabetically by the author's last name.

For books, include the author's name, the year of publication, the title of the work, the place published and the name of the publisher:

Steffensen, V. (2020). Fire Country: How Indigenous Fire Management Could Help Save Australia. Melbourne: Hardie Grant Explore.

For a website, include the author (or organisation), the year of publication, the title of the article or page, the website name, and a link to the URL:

Paltridge, R. and Young, A. (2016). 'The spark of life: how fire defines a desert country'. Country Needs People. Available at: https://www.countryneedspeople.org.au/the_spark_of_life

Book-length informational texts

Some informational texts are whole books, such as Bruce Pascoe's *Dark Emu* which explores the agricultural practices of First Nations cultures in Australia. Writing a book-length informational text allows a writer to explore their topic in greater detail. In addition to headings and subheadings, a book-length informational text will use chapters to organise information and will typically provide a contents page and index to help readers locate information easily.

In 2019, Bruce Pascoe released *Young Dark Emu*, an edition of his book designed to share this information with younger readers. Read the following extract from Young *Dark Emu*.

Chapter 6 [extract]: Fire

Aboriginal people burned specific areas of land every few years, rotating three different areas from year to year. They timed the burning around particular seasons and weather conditions. This approach controlled the intensity of fires and allowed animals and plants to survive in surrounding areas.

The complex system had several benefits, including adding nutrients to the soil and keeping areas clear for farming. Within days of the fires, fresh green shoots would sprout. This attracted animals, making it easier for Aboriginal people to hunt.

Aboriginal people learned over thousands of years how to use fire effectively and safely. Jinoor Jack, an Aboriginal man from East Gippsland, shared his knowledge with emancipated convict, Robert Alexander. He told Alexander that every five years in February or March he should burn the land:

... after the longest day when the sap begins to go down. In that period there are westerly winds in the morning that change to northeast in the afternoon, which provide natural back burn.

Source: O'Conner, N. and K.A. Jones (2003)

Unfortunately, most Europeans did not value Aboriginal knowledge. When Aboriginal people were forced from their lands, and the European settlers used their own farming methods, the effect of these changes was fast and devastating.

10.4 Check for understanding

1 What is the purpose of this informational text?

___

2 How does the purpose of this text differ from the report earlier in this unit?

___

___

3 Does this text use the same academic style as the report? In what ways is it similar and different?

___

___

Websites

A website is another type of informational text. In 2021, the 'Australia: State of the Environment 2021' report was published. It brought together scientific, traditional and cultural knowledge to assess the state of Australia's environment and to make recommendations for future actions. It was then transformed into an interactive website to share its findings with all Australians.

10.5 Reflecting and discussing

Discuss the following questions in pairs, in small groups or with the whole class as directed by your teacher.

1. As a digital text, the website uses features such as drop-down menus, carousels, breadcrumb trails, a search function, arrows and icon buttons to help readers navigate the information. Find examples of each and discuss which features you find most useful.
2. This website can be considered a **hybrid text**, incorporating the report itself plus Aboriginal and Torres Strait Islander artworks, infographics, animations and videos. What benefits do you think come from including information in such a variety of ways?
3. What advantages does a website have over a printed report in terms of helping to inform readers?
4. Which type of text would you prefer to use to find information on a topic: a report, a book or a website? Explain your choice.

hybrid text A composite text resulting from a purposeful mixing of elements from different sources or genres (e.g. 'infotainment')

Infographics

An infographic is a visual representation of information or data that is designed to make it easier to understand and digest. It can combine text, images, charts, graphs and other visual elements to present complex information in a clear and engaging way. Infographics are created with the purpose of quickly communicating key facts, statistics or ideas to the viewer.

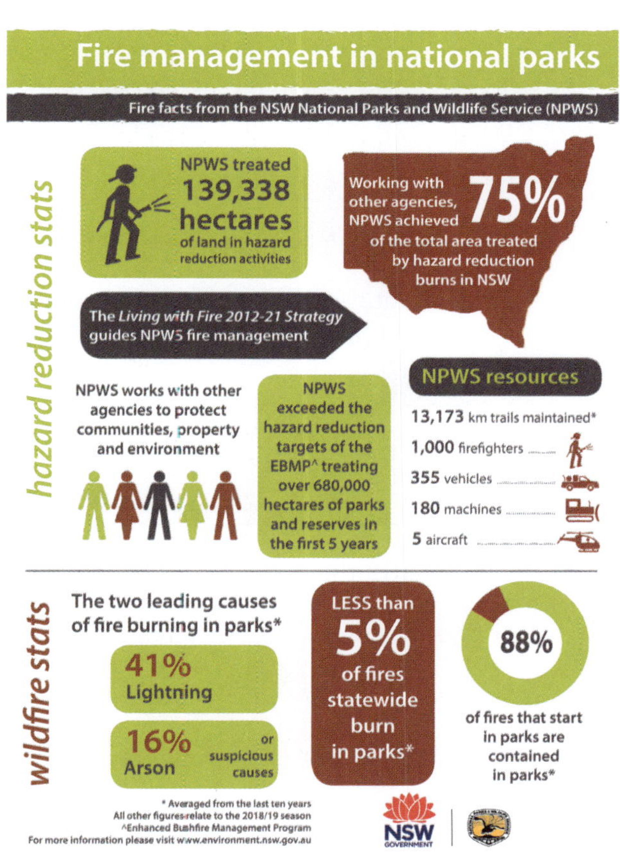

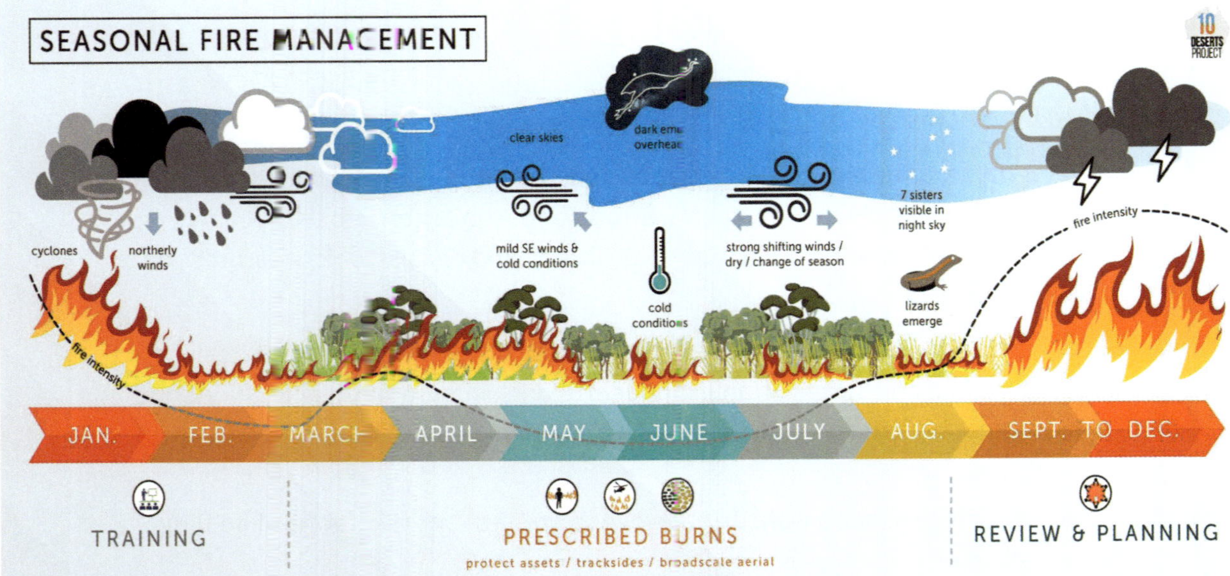

9.3 Check for understanding

1 According to the 'Seasonal fire management' infographic:

a When is the best time to conduct prescribed burns?

____

b What is the weather like at the beginning of the year? How can you tell?

____

2 According to the 'Fire management in national parks' infographic:

a What proportion of New South Wales national parks were treated with hazard reduction burns in 2018/19?

____

b What are the leading causes of fires in national parks?

____

3 Circle which of the following visual elements are used in the infographics:

photographs	illustrations	timelines	
cross-sections	tables	maps	
graphs	diagrams	icons	logos

10.7 Get creative

1 Using the information from the report on Aboriginal fire practices, as well the excerpt from chapter 6 of *Young Dark Emu*, create an infographic that informs readers about this traditional land management tool. Alternatively, create an infographic on another topic that you are interested in.

2 Write a brief report about your favourite hobby, or even a band or television show you like. Use the following steps to help you.

a Identify a purpose for your report. What topic would you like to inform people about?

b Identify key subtopics. For example, in a report on Australian Rules Football, you might consider subtopics such as the origins of the sport, key rules and characteristics, the role of the AFL, grassroots clubs, and the sport's position within Australian culture. Use these subtopics to create clear subheadings for your report.

c Conduct some research, making sure you use trustworthy sources and keep a record of the texts you use in your report.

d Draft your report, with:

- a clear introduction that explains the **context** and purpose of your report
- a body with subtopics organised under appropriate subheadings
- a conclusion that summarises your findings and adds a final comment.

e Include some kind of visual element, such as a chart, graph or illustration, to add to your explanations.

f **Edit** your report to ensure that you have written in an academic style and have included some appropriately cited references to your research sources.

context An environment or situation (social, cultural or historical) in which a text is responded to or created. Or wording surrounding an unfamiliar word, which a reader or listener uses to understand its meaning
edit To prepare, alter, adapt or refine with attention to grammar, spelling, punctuation and vocabulary

UNIT 11

Using comprehension strategies

Every day, you will come across a range of texts that you will need to comprehend. To 'comprehend' something means to understand and make meaning from it. These texts that you are required to understand might include an advertisement on television, a recipe for dinner, a train timetable, an explanation in a textbook, a webpage, a chapter of a novel you're reading, or the feed on a social media site. Clearly, comprehension plays a vital role in all of our lives on a daily basis. Well-developed comprehension skills allow us to function easily rather than living in a state of complete confusion.

In this unit you will learn:

- about different comprehension strategies
- to practise using different comprehension strategies for a range of text forms
- to use comprehension strategies to enhance your understanding and enjoyment of texts.

Curriculum content

Australian Curriculum content description	Content code
Identify and use vocabulary typical of academic texts.	AC9E8LA08
Use comprehension strategies such as visualising, predicting, connecting, summarising, monitoring, questioning and inferring to interpret and evaluate ideas in texts.	AC9E8LY05

What are comprehension strategies?

comprehension strategies Processes used by readers to make meaning from texts. They include activating and using prior knowledge, predicting likely future events in a text, monitoring meaning and critically reflecting

Comprehension strategies are the specific processes we use to make sense of texts so that we can understand them. This unit will particularly draw your attention to the following comprehension skills:

Each of these strategies is explained separately below. However, it is important to remember that often you will use more than one strategy at the same time to comprehend a text. Indeed, the **Check for understanding** and **Reflecting and discussing** activities throughout Units 1–10 of this book integrate a range of different comprehension strategies simultaneously.

In this unit, the comprehension strategies that are a particular focus in each section are indicated before the activities commence. This will help you to be aware of the specific processes you are using in each activity.

Summary of common comprehension strategies

Skimming is reading quickly in order to get a general overview of a text. It only allows for an overall impression of the text but is a very useful strategy in helping you decide what kind of text you are reading and identifying its main topic.

Scanning involves reading quickly in order to find specific facts, words or phrases. This strategy requires you to move your eyes quickly down the text to find only the information that will answer a particular question.

Activating prior knowledge requires you to think about what you already know to help you understand a new text. It may involve you brainstorming what you already know about a text's main topic or making connections with something similar you have already read.

Visualising involves forming a mental image or picture in your head to illustrate what you are reading.

Predicting involves making a logical presumption about what might happen next in a text, often based on prior experience of similar texts.

Connecting is about making links between the text you are trying to understand and other texts. It also involves thinking about how the text relates to you and to the world at large.

Summarising involves choosing only the most important information in a text and then rewriting it in shortened form.

Questioning refers to asking yourself questions before, during or after reading a text, in ways that help you think more deeply about what you are reading and help clarify your understanding.

Inferring means making a deduction about what something might mean. Even though a text might not state something specifically, you will be able to draw logical conclusions based on the clues or hints it offers and through your skills of reasoning.

Comprehension focus 1: scanning, summarising and inferring

On 4 June 1940, the British Prime Minister at the time, Winston Churchill, made his memorable 'We Shall Fight on the Beaches' speech. It was one of the defining speeches of World War II. This speech sent a powerful message to the enemy – Nazi Germany – and brought together the United Kingdom during one of its most testing times.

We Shall Fight on the Beaches

I have, myself, full confidence that if all do their duty, if nothing is neglected, and if the best arrangements are made, as they are being made, we shall prove ourselves once again able to defend our Island home, to ride out the storm of war, and to outlive the menace of tyranny, if necessary for years, if necessary alone. At any rate, that is what we are going to try to do. That is the resolve of His Majesty's Government – every man of them. That is the will of Parliament and the nation. The British Empire and the French Republic, linked together in their cause and in their need, will defend to the death their native soil, aiding each other like good comrades to the utmost of their strength. Even though large tracts of Europe and many old and famous States have fallen or may fall into the grip of the Gestapo and all the odious apparatus of Nazi rule, we shall not flag or fail. We shall go on to the end, we shall fight in France, we shall fight on the seas and oceans, we shall fight with growing confidence and growing strength in the air, we shall defend our Island, whatever the cost may be, we shall fight on the beaches, we shall fight on the landing grounds, we shall fight in the fields and in the streets, we shall fight in the hills; we shall never surrender, and even if, which I do not for a moment believe, this Island or a large part of it were subjugated and starving, then our Empire beyond the seas, armed and guarded by the British Fleet, would carry on the struggle, until, in God's good time, the New World, with all its power and might, steps forth to the rescue and the liberation of the old.

11.1

Activity

1 What do you believe is the main **purpose** of this speech?

- a to prepare British citizens for the possibility of losing the war ☐
- b to send an aggressive message to the enemy ☐
- c to lift civilian morale in Great Britain ☐
- d to announce an alliance with France ☐
- e to admit defeat in the war ☐

2 The first sentence of the speech is very long. Rewrite it in more concise sentences without losing the meaning.

____

____

3 Identify some of the negative descriptions of the enemy and their behaviour.

____

____

____

4 What is the effect of including these descriptions?

____

____

____

5 Who is Churchill referring to when he says 'our Empire beyond the seas' and 'the New World'?

____

____

6 Which of the following persuasive devices are used in the speech? Refer to (Chapter 2) for a reminder of these persuasive devices.

- a imperatives and calls to action ☐
- b inclusive language ☐
- c emotive language ☐
- d metaphors and similes ☐
- e appeal to **values** ☐

purpose An intended or assumed reason for a type of text
values Ideas and beliefs specific to individuals and groups

Comprehension focus 2: scanning, activating prior knowledge, connecting and questioning

The following text is a mock-news article published by the satirical website, *The Shovel*.

Dog Descended From Wild Animals May Die If Not Fed $80-A-Bag Food

A small dog whose ancestors survived for thousands of years on scraps and raw meat can only stomach a scientifically-developed mix of organic chicken liver and cracked pearled barley.

The dog, named Joseph, told reporters today that he was allergic to wheat, leftover sausages, some proteins, and any food costing less than $10 a kilo. 'It's a hereditary thing,' he said.

Joseph – a member of the canine group of species – said his food had an exclusively-designed texture that encouraged chewing and promoted digestion. 'It has a clinically proven formula to produce a healthy immune system and promote good bacteria – just like my ancestors would have eaten. It's the balanced diet I need for my rigorous lifestyle,' he said, before heading off for a nap.

Offered a leftover chop, Joseph said it was "too risky'. 'Are you mad? Do you even know what's in that thing? Who knows what that could do to my coat, let alone my skin condition?" he said.

Joseph says that, just like his great-great-great-great grandfather, he strictly eats 1.25 cups of food a day.

11.2 Activity

1 What main point do you think the writer of the article is trying to make about the way people treat their pets?

____

____

2 The article uses technical vocabulary that we expect to find in credible academic or formal texts, such as:

scientifically-developed	hereditary	exclusively-designed
clinically proven formula	rigorous lifestyle	

a **Scan** the article and highlight the technical words and phrases above when you find them.

b What is the purpose of using this type of vocabulary in the article?

____

____

c Circle the other kinds of texts that use vocabulary typical of academic texts below.

text message to a friend	short story	analytical essay
memoir	research paper	scientific journal

scan To read, moving eyes quickly down a page, seeking specific words and phrases. It is also used when a reader first finds information to determine whether it will answer their questions

Comprehension focus 3: scanning, skimming and summarising

The following text is an extract from *The Hunger Games*, a 2008 dystopian novel by Suzanne Collins.

Just as the town clock strikes two, the mayor steps up to the podium and begins to read. It's the same story every year. He tells of the history of Panem, the country that rose up out of the ashes of a place that was once called North America. He lists the disasters, the droughts, the storms, the fires, the encroaching seas that swallowed up so much of the land, the brutal war for what little sustenance remained. The result was Panem, a shining Capitol ringed by thirteen districts, which brought peace and prosperity to its citizens. Then came the Dark Days, the uprising of the districts against the Capitol. Twelve were defeated, the thirteenth obliterated. The Treaty of Treason gave us the new laws to guarantee peace and, as our yearly reminder that the Dark Days must never be repeated, it gave us the Hunger Games.

The rules of the Hunger Games are simple. In punishment for the uprising, each of the twelve districts must provide one girl and one boy, called tributes, to participate. The twenty-four tributes will be imprisoned in a vast outdoor arena that could hold anything from a burning desert to a frozen wasteland. Over a period of several weeks, the competitors must fight to the death. The last tribute standing wins.

11.3

Activity

1 **Skim** the extract and circle the features below that tell you what sort of text it is.

setting persuasive language characterisation

rhetorical questions statistics

2 List all the reality television programs you can think of.

____

____

____

3 One of the **themes** explored in *The Hunger Games* is the ethics of reality TV and, in particular, whether it is morally right or wrong to watch people suffering as entertainment. Are there any reality TV shows that you think cross some kind of ethical line or do you think they should go further?

____

____

____

skim Reading quickly, selecting key words and details through a text to determine the general meaning or main messages or ideas

theme The main idea, concept or message of a text

Comprehension focus 4: summarising and visualising

The image below is from *Quotations from Chairman Mao Tse-Tung*, also known as *The Little Red Book*. The text was very popular amongst the Chinese during China's Cultural Revolution (1966–1976). The text at the bottom of the poster loosely translates as: 'Advance courageously along the glorious road of Chairman Mao's "May 7 Directive".'

11.4

Activity

1 What kind of people are depicted in the poster? Consider what their actions and appearance tell us about them.

____

____

2 Summarise what is happening in the background of the poster.

____

____

3 What is the feeling or mood associated with the poster?

____

____

4 Summarise the overall meaning or message of the poster.

____

____

5 Images such as posters and photographs often use **symbolism** to create meaning. What symbols are used in this poster? Think about colour, costume, landmarks etc.

____

____

6 Imagine you were designing a poster to celebrate an Australian achievement. What symbols could you use to show this Australian **context**?

____

____

symbolism The use of one object, person or situation to signify or represent another, by giving them meanings that are different from their literal sense (e.g. a dove is a symbol of peace)
context An environment or situation (social, cultural or historical) in which a text is responded to or created. Or wording surrounding an unfamiliar word, which a reader or listener uses to understand its meaning

Comprehension focus 5: activating prior knowledge, questioning, predicting and connecting

Kirsty Murray's historical novel *Bridie's Fire* is set between1848 and 1852 in Ireland and

Australia. While the novel is based on the true history of the Great Famine (also known as the Potato Famine) in Ireland, the story is fictional.

11.5.1

Activity

1 What do you know about famines? Whom do they mostly affect and where? Are there famines in the world right now?

____

____

____

2 Based on the introductory description, what kind of characters do you think the novel will be about?

____

____

Read the following extract from *Bridie's Fire.*

The next morning was bright and clear. Bridie woke with Brandon and Paddy a tangle of limbs and tousled hair on the pallet beside her. The O'Farrell children were gone. Someone must have woken them quietly and then moved Bridie and her brothers to their bed.

The chicken that they kept in the cupboard was scratching and clucking, anxious to be out in the day. Bridie padded across the pressed-earth floor, reached in between the wooden bars of the cage under the cupboard and drew a warm egg from beneath the hen.

The door to the cottage was open, and the fire was smouldering on the hearth. She wondered why Mam and Dad hadn't woken her when they left and why her mother hadn't let the chicken out. Still clutching the warm hen's egg in her hand, she stepped over the threshold. Pale dawn light crept across the morning sky. Bridie walked around the back of the cottage to where the family potato plot lay. Her parents were already at work in the field, but there was something odd about the way they were going about it, a frenzied desperation in their movements. Then Bridie saw that the leaves of the plants looked strange, limp and wilted. The day before they had been a thick tangle of stalks and rich green leaves.

Then, as her father dug his hands into the black soil, he moaned, a horrible low growl like a wounded dog.

'Da, don't!' she called, frightened.

He looked up, his face white and contorted with despair. 'It's the blight, girl.'

11.5.2

Activity

1 What questions do you have about what you have read so far? Are there words in the extract that you don't understand?

___

___

Keep reading …

Bridie caught her breath and pressed her fists against her cheeks. She knew what this could mean. She had seen the gaunt and desperate men and women, turned out of home when their crops failed and they'd been unable to pay their rent. They drifted across the land and wound their way around the peninsula, begging at every door, driven by a hungry wind. All across the country, first in the north, and then rapidly spreading south, the potato harvest had been hit by a terrible cholera, but the O'Connors had been spared – until now.

11.5.3

Activity

1 Have any of questions you recorded in the previous activity been answered yet? Are there any words you still don't understand? If so, use a dictionary to find their meanings and record them in the space below.

___

___

2 What do you **predict** will happen in the story now? Give reasons for your prediction.

___

___

3 What indications are there that the novel is set in Ireland?

___

___

___

___

predicting An informed presumption about something that might happen. Predicting at the text level can include working out what a text might contain based on previous knowledge of the type of text

4 Find Ireland on a world map. How far away is it from Australia?

5 Summarise the sort of life Bridie and her family have in this extract.

Comprehension focus 6: scanning, skimming, summarising and visualising

The following extract is the first poem of *Bindi*, a verse novel written by Kirli Saunders.

Being Bindi

At school
on the first day
they split us into groups
to learn about our new classmates

When they ask

I say:

'Wedayo, my name is Bindi Hoskins
I'm 11 years old

I live with Mum and Dad
And a Brother and a Sister

We live on the hill
up a steep driveway
in a yellow house
backing onto bushland
at number 19.

Nan and Pop
live close by.

We have
two dogs:
Rocky and Tazz.

And two horses:
Nelly and Scoot (my one is Nell)

And chickens
And rabbits.

But mostly
you'll find me
on an adventure
with my friends
Olive, Henry and Marco –

that's if I'm not playing hockey
or painting ...'

Mr Milburn smiles and nods

and it's someone else's turn.

11.6 **Activity**

1 Scan the text and explain what makes it a poem (verse).

2 Explain the difference between prose and verse. You may need to do some research.

3 In one sentence, summarise what happens in the poem.

4 What is the name of the persona or speaker of the poem?

5 How many siblings does she have?

6 Find or draw an image that visually captures one of the descriptions in the poem.

Comprehension focus 7: activating prior knowledge, questioning, predicting and inferring

Read the following extract from Ying Chang Compestine's novel, *Revolution Is Not a Dinner Party*.

> Mother picked up a stack of old newspapers from beside the stove. Carefully, she checked every page before laying it around a stool, setting two sheets with Chairman Mao's pictures on the counter. Months earlier, a nurse had been sent to prison as an anti-Maoist just because she lit her stove with a newspaper page with Mao's photo on it.

11.7.1

Activity

1 Tick the questions you have about the text so far.

a Who is Chairman Mao? ☐

b What is an anti-Maoist? ☐

c Why would someone be sent to prison just for lighting a stove with newspaper pages with photos on them? ☐

2 Activate your prior knowledge to answer these questions; otherwise, see if you can find answers for them online.

____

____

____

3 What inference can you make about this text's setting so far? Where and when do you think the story is set?

____

____

Now read this extract from *Revolution Is Not a Dinner Party.*

> I noticed a cloth rice sack in the corner next to some herbal medicine bottles, and folded clothes. 'Why are you packing, Mom?'
>
> 'When they come for us, I want to be ready.' She led me to the stool and raked her hard-toothed comb through my hair.
>
> As each stroke yanked my hair, pain shot through my lice-chewed body. I clenched my teeth, not wanting to cry out. Were we going to a labor camp? Before knowing that they kept Father in the jail nearby, I had wished they would send us to his camp, wherever it was. Now I didn't want to leave. I wanted to be here in case they ever brought him back to the hospital.

11.7.2

Activity

1 What inference can you make about why the narrator's father is being kept in a jail nearby?

____

____

Keep reading …

Something cold drizzled through my hair. Within a second, my scalp burned. 'I hope this will kill the lice,' Mother whispered. Her ox-bone comb scraped against my raw scalp.

I couldn't endure any more of the pain and the itching. 'You are hurting me!' I shouted.

Mother stopped.

Stiffening my back, I waited for her to scold me for raising my voice and showing disrespect.

A moment later, she whispered, 'Ling, your hair is too thick. The coal oil can't kill all the lice.' She put down her comb and left the room.

Hadn't she heard me shouting? What was she planning to do now?

Mother returned with a pair of scissors and Father's razor. 'We have to shave your head.'

I jumped off the chair. 'No! There must be another way!'

She took a step back. 'I don't know what else to do, Ling. I used up this month's ration. I even emptied the lamp. If I don't cut your hair, the lice will spread throughout the apartment.' She tilted the blue oil cup, showing me it was empty. We received two cups of coal oil each month. Without the oil, we'd have to live in the dark for the rest of the month.

11.7.3

Activity

1 What are your predictions about the events that will now happen in the novel?

____

____

____

2 What inferences can you make about the quality of life for Ling and her mother based on the evidence in the extract? Give reasons for your answer.

____

____

____

____

3 What is the effect of the first-person narrative **point of view** ('I', 'we') in the passage, rather than third-person narrative point of view?

___

___

___

4 Why do you think Ying Chang Compestine wrote this novel?

___

___

point of view The position from which the text is designed to be perceived (e.g. a narrator might take a role of first or third person, omniscient or restricted in knowledge of events or the opinion presented in a text)

Comprehension focus 8: activating prior knowledge and connecting

The following extract is from an interview conducted with Henry Gibson Dan, popularly known as 'Seaman Dan', on the ABC's *Message Stick* program. Seaman Dan is a singer-songwriter from the Torres Strait Islands.

Seaman Dan: Ever since I was 16 years old I worked on a trochus lugger. I've been at sea most of my life, so they call me 'Seaman'. Seaman Dan. My proper name is Henry Gibson Dan but everybody knows me as Seaman Dan. Because I belong to the sea.

Living in the Torres Straits we have a happy lifestyle. Thursday Island, well, I would describe it as a tropical paradise. The water is emerald-blue and golden sands. We're a multicultural society and the lifestyle is very much laid-back. I suppose this is why all of my songs, they've got that laid-back sound ...

I was born on Thursday Island, 25th of August 1929 at the general hospital ... My great-grandfather, he comes from Kingston, Jamaica. He came over on a London Missionary Society vessel with seven missionaries, and they landed at Darnley Island, it's the most eastern island from Thursday Island. They landed there on the 1st of July 1871. Christianity was brought to the Torres Strait on that particular day. And since then we've always looked towards that day, respected that day, we call it 'Coming Of The Light'.

11.8

Activity

1 List the things you already know about the Torres Straight Islands (e.g. location, culture, traditions)

____

____

2 This interview transcript highlights Dan's interesting and distinctive voice. Circle all of the words below that you think describe Dan's voice. Look up the definitions of any words you don't understand.

conversational	formal	laconic	relaxed
friendly	thoughtful	sad	irritated
meandering	reflective	blunt	

3 In full sentences, describe Dan's voice using at least two of the words you chose above. Include quotes from the interview to support your view.

____

____

____

4 Think about how Dan's life experiences are similar to or different from your own by completing the following sentences and comparing your responses to Dan's in the extract.

Ever since I was __________ years old I ______________________________

____.

My proper name is __________ but everybody knows me as __________.

Living in ______________ we have a ______________ lifestyle.

I was born in/on______________, __________ (date) at ______________.

My grandparents came from ______________________________.

Comprehension focus 9: summarising and connecting

The three images below form part of a social media campaign released during the Coronavirus pandemic.

visual features Visual components of a text which may include placement, salience, framing, representation of action or reaction, shot size, social distance and camera angle

Image 1

Image 2

Image 3

11.9

Activity

1 Summarise the main purpose of the images.

____

____

2 What features of the images tell you that the text forms part of a social media campaign?

____

3 What **visual features** do all of the images have in common?

____

____

____

4 Do you think the images portray a realistic representation of staying home during the pandemic? Consider a range of experiences, including your own.

____

____

____

____

Comprehension focus 10: scanning and inferring

The following extract is from the website of Centre of the Cell, a science education centre based at Queen Mary, University of London.

Animal experiments help scientists understand diseases that afflict animals and humans. Scientists also use animal experiments to test new treatments for human and animal diseases, for example new medicines or new surgical techniques. Finally, some animal experiments help scientists understand the basic biology of animals.

Animals get similar diseases to humans and these sick animals can be used in experiments. Animals can also be treated in certain ways or be bred so that they develop certain diseases. For example, if cancer cells grown in the laboratory are injected into mice, the mice develop cancer.

...

An animal with a disease can be used to test new medicines. The scientists want to find out if the new treatment works and if it has any side effects. Sometimes, blood samples are taken to measure substances and reactions in the body. Other animals may be used to try out new surgical techniques, for instance those used in transplanting organs.

11.10

Activity

1 Which of the following words describe the tone of this text? Circle them.

serious	angry	friendly	logical	hostile
casual	informal	informative	scholarly	relaxed

2 Record a definition for the term 'academic text'.

____

____

3 Write a list of text types or forms that could be considered academic.

____

____

4 Highlight the vocabulary used throughout the extract that is typical of an academic text that has been written by professionals in the scientific field.

5 What can you infer is the viewpoint of the writers of this extract? Select one of the following options.

a Animal experimentation is cruel and should be stopped immediately. ☐

b Animal experimentation for the purpose of scientific and medical progress is justified. ☐

Improving your writing

This unit targets the knowledge and skills that will help improve the quality of your writing. Each activity is designed to help you revise or learn about a particular **language feature** or grammar **convention**. Understanding the different parts of speech – such as nouns and adjectives – and the way sentences are structured will enable you to communicate clearly with readers. There are lots of opportunities for you to apply your understanding of literacy and language in the writing activities of this unit. You will also be given prompts to practise editing sample sentences and paragraphs.

language features Features that support meaning (e.g. clause- and word-level grammar, vocabulary, figurative language, punctuation, images). Choices vary for the purpose, subject matter, audience and mode or medium

convention An accepted practice that has developed over time and is generally used and understood (e.g. use of punctuation)

Curriculum content

Australian Curriculum content description	Content code
Understand the effect of nominalisation in texts.	AC9E8LA06
Understand and use punctuation conventions including semicolons and dashes to extend ideas and support meaning.	AC9E8LA09
Create and edit literary texts that experiment with language features and literary devices for particular purposes and effects.	AC9E8LE06
Apply learnt knowledge to spell accurately and to learn new words.	AC9E8LY08

Nouns

Nouns are naming words. Nouns name objects, people, places, groups and emotions. There are five types of nouns.

noun A word class that includes all words denoting person, place, object or thing, idea or emotion. Nouns may be common, proper, collective, abstract and compound

Type of noun	What it names	Examples
common (countable and uncountable)	ordinary things	countable: people, cars, trees uncountable: water, air, music
proper	particular things, including people and places	Australia, Canberra, Anthony Albanese
collective	groups of things	flock (group of sheep), team (group of football players), galaxy (group of stars)
concrete	physical things you can see, touch, smell, hear or taste	flower, horizon, song
abstract	ideas, qualities and emotions that cannot be seen or touched	jealousy, beauty, ego

12.1 Activity

1 Sort these nouns into the correct categories in the table below

fish calmness gang cutlery friendship
Roald Dahl vegetable milk Jupiter library
honesty candle furniture forest France

Common noun	Proper nouns	Collective nouns	Abstract nouns
Countable			
Uncountable			

2 Rewrite the following passage with correct capitalisation for the common and proper nouns.

jayden had wanted to go and see uluru for as long as he could remember. He often talked to his aunt hilda and uncle martin about his Dream to go there, because they visited alice springs only last year and had seen uluru for themselves during their Trip. Although his Parents had promised to take him to see the eiffel tower in paris next august, it was the attraction in australia that jayden wanted to see even more.

Adjectives

Adjectives describe or modify nouns by giving additional information about them. For example:

» the bright, clear morning

» the morning was bright and clear.

Adjectives provide 'colour' to a piece of writing. They help to make characters and settings come to life by creating pictures in the minds of readers. They also help to make the description more precise and specific.

adjective A word class that describes, identifies or quantifies a noun or a pronoun, e.g. two (number or quantity), my (possessive), ancient (descriptive), shorter (comparative), wooden (classifying)

12.2 Activity

1 Underline the adjectives in the following sentences. Look up definitions for any unfamiliar words.

a It was such a picturesque view that she had to take a photo with her new camera.

b She was immediately besotted by the cute, brown puppy.

c The lettuce was inedible as it was limp and wilted.

2 There is a wealth of adjectives to describe degrees of temperature, other than just 'hot' and 'cold'. The table below shows some of them.

freezing	toasty	lukewarm	cosy	chilly
scorching	glacial	sweltering	mild	tepid
frigid	warm	crisp	icy	balmy

Rank these adjectives from coldest to hottest. Some may be approximately equal to others.

3 Choose from the list above to complete the following sentences.

a It was a ________________ summer night so we slept under the stars.

b Winters in England are ________________.

c The bathwater had cooled down and was now ________________.

Phrases and clauses

Phrases and **clauses** relate to the organisation and expression of ideas. A phrase is a group of words that does not contain both a **subject** (a person or thing doing an action) and a **verb**, so it does not make sense on its own. Some examples of phrases are:

» some noisy students (no verb)

» after the terrible movie (no verb)

» frolicking in the field, laughing hysterically (no subject)

A clause is a group of words with a subject and a verb. Every sentence needs to include at least one clause. Some examples of clauses are:

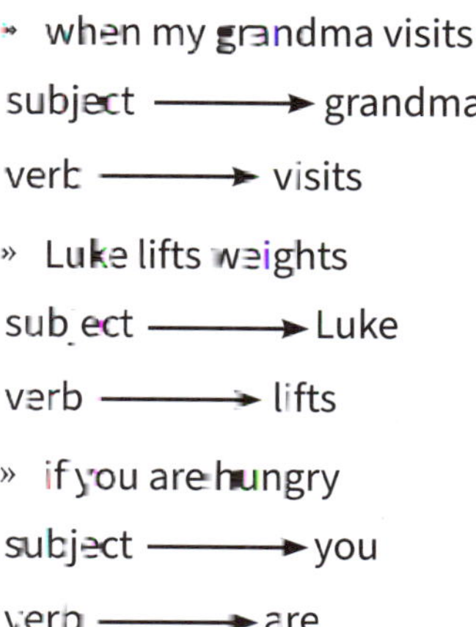

phrase A group of words often beginning with a preposition but without a subject and verb combination (e.g. 'on the river'; 'with brown eyes')
clause A grammatical unit referring to a happening or state e.g. 'the team won' (happening), 'the dog is red' (state), usually containing a subject and a verb group/phrase
subject A word or group of words (usually a noun group/phrase) in a sentence or clause representing the person, thing or idea doing the action that follows (e.g. 'The dog [subject] was barking')
verb A word class that expresses processes that include doing, feeling, thinking, saying and relating

Main clauses

A main (or independent) clause can stand alone; that is, it makes sense as a complete sentence by itself. The following examples are main clauses because they could also be full sentences.

» We made a cake

» My sister likes picking flowers

» I'm going to the shops

Subordinate clauses

A subordinate (or dependent) clause can't stand alone, because it doesn't make sense by itself. The following subordinate clauses could follow on from the three examples above but they could not be sentences by themselves.

» because it was Dad's birthday

» which can sometimes make us late for school

» after I have a shower

When you combine a main clause and a subordinate clause, you form a **complex sentence.** If you put the main clause first, you don't need to use a comma to separate it from the subordinate clause unless the main clause is very long. For example:

complex sentence A sentence with one or more subordinate clauses. In the following example, the subordinate clause is shown in brackets: I took my umbrella [because it was raining]

» We made a cake because it was Dad's birthday.

main clause → We made a cake

subordinate clause → because it was Dad's birthday

If you put the subordinate clause first, you do need to use a comma after it. For example:

» Because it was Dad's birthday, we made a cake.

subordinate clause → because it was Dad's birthday

main clause → We made a cake

12.3

Activity

1 Are the following groups of words phrases or clauses? Write P for phrase or C for clause in each box.

a the world being slowly transformed into a wilderness ☐

b in a book somewhere ☐

c I must hold on to my ideals ☐

2 Circle the main clauses and underline the subordinate clauses in the following sentences.

a The dog ran away when it heard the thunder.

b Since it was the last day of term, we had a class party.

c It was bad weather so the athletics day was postponed.

3 Join these clauses to form complex sentences, remembering to use a comma if required.

a [the phone rang] + [just as we were sitting down to dinner]

____

b [because it was so hot] + [we bought ice-creams]

____

Embedded clauses

One clause can sometimes be embedded into another to create a full sentence. The embedded clause adds more information and expands on the idea introduced by the sentence. For example:

» The students attend school in the city.

» The students, who travel by bus from their home country town, attend school in the city.

12.4

Activity

1 Rewrite the following clauses so that the information from the second clause is embedded in the first clause, making one full sentence. You will need to change or omit some words to achieve correct sentence structure.

a Anne is an excellent cook. She is also an outstanding musician.

____

b The car screeched to a halt. The car was a green Toyota.

____

c The hotel was very luxurious. It was located in the heart of the city.

____

Nominalisation

Nominalisation involves making an adjective or verb into a noun. Often the noun is abstract.

The following are examples of nominalisation, where adjectives or verbs have been turned into nouns.

adjective	noun (after the process of nomi-nalisation)
beautiful	beauty
wealthy	wealth
happy	happiness

verb	noun (after the process of nomi-nalisation)
confess	confession
discover	discovery
achieve	achievement

12.5

Activity

1 Change the following words into nouns by nominalising them.

a divide ____________ b experiment ____________

c attractive ____________ d devoted ____________

e weak ____________ f dangerous ____________

Nominalisation has the effect of enhancing the sophistication of your writing and eliminating unnecessary words. Practice in nominalisation will also help to improve your vocabulary.

2 Find definitions for the following nominalised words and add the words they have been made from. An example has been provided for you.

Nominalisation	Definition	nominalised word
adaptation	the process of changing or being altered into another form or to suit a different environment	adapt
implication		
expansion		
variation		
admission		

Apostrophes

Apostrophes have two functions: to signal possession (ownership) and **contraction** (missing letters).

contraction An abbreviated version of a word or words, often formed by shortening a word or merging 2 words into one (e.g. doctor: Dr; do not: don't)

Possession

The apostrophe is used to show who or what something belongs to.

Type of noun	How to form possessive	Example
singular	add 's	The Prime Minister's speech
plural ending in s or es	add '	the berries' colour the cities' citizens
plural not ending in s	add 's	the children's clothes

Contraction

The apostrophe is used to show that a word has been shortened and that there are letters missing.

Non-contracted forms	Contraction
it is, there is	it's, there's
I will, you will, it will	I'll, you'll, it'll
cannot	can't
could have, should have	could've, should've

12.6

Activity

1 Write the following words as contractions

a they had ______________________

b does not ______________________

c of the clock ______________________

d what is ______________________

e how is ______________________

2 Form the possessives for the following family names (surnames). An example has been done for you.

The Smiths' house is for sale. (Smith family)

a The ____________________ new dog barks a lot. (Healey family)

b The ____________________ car was stolen. (Lee family)

c I'm collecting ____________________________________ mail while he is on holiday. (Mr Brown)

d The ____________________ garden is looking terrific. (Nguyen family)

Dashes

A dash is a punctuation mark with many different uses. Many people confuse the dash (–) with the much shorter hyphen (-), but dashes are used differently.

A dash is used for three main purposes:

» to show a really quick change in the direction of ideas (for example, 'I mentioned before that she won the award – but that's not what we're supposed to be discussing!')

» to set apart and emphasise additional information when the sentence would still make sense without it (for example, 'I ate the doughnut – the big, chocolate one – because I didn't know it was yours!')

» to show a span of numbers, time or distance (for example, 'I am hoping to transfer to a specialist arts school for Years 10–12').

When you use dashes to set apart information, a pair of dashes can be replaced by parentheses (rounded brackets). For example:

» The school isn't open at that time on Mondays, Tuesdays, Wednesday and Thursdays – or Sundays for that matter – so you will have to study at the public library down the road.

» The school isn't open at that time on Mondays, Tuesdays, Wednesday and Thursdays (or Sundays for that matter) so you will have to study at the public library down the road.

The main difference between parentheses and dashes is that a dash will often put extra emphasis on the additional information, while a bracket tends to make it less important. You can insert a dash with the 'insert symbol' function of your PC (or Ctrl+minus key on a numerical keyboard) or by holding down option and the minus keys on a Mac. You should never use more than one pair of dashes in a sentence.

12.7

Activity

1 Read the extract from Taylor Mali's poem 'Totally like whatever, you know?' below and identify the reason that dashes have been used.

> Declarative sentences – so-called
> because they used to, like, DECLARE things to be true, okay,
> as opposed to other things are, like, totally, you know, not –
> have been infected by a totally hip
> and tragically cool interrogative tone? You know?

Reason for dashes: ____

____

2 Add dashes in the correct places in the following sentences and explain the reason for using the dash in each situation.

a I can't wait to go on holidays we're going to Cairns because I really need a break.

Reason for dashes: ____

____

b You know I was the top of my class in maths are you listening?

Reason for dashes: ____

____

c Tai kept on talking about noodles I normally prefer pasta to rice noodles so we had to get them for lunch.

Reason for dashes: ____

____

d Hey you with the blue cap on come here right now!

Reason for dashes: ____

____

e It was so noisy everyone was talking all at once that I could hardly hear my own thoughts.

Reason for dashes: ______________________________

____

3 Rewrite these sentences using dashes for the spans of numbers.

a I won my school's 100 metres sprint award in 2009, 2010, 2011, 2012 and 2013.

____

b Harry Potter is my favourite series, but I like books 2, 3, 4 and 5 the best.

____

c My favourite years of school were Year 4, Year 5 and Year 6.

____

Confusing word pairs

The table below is made up of commonly mixed up words.

12.8

Activity

Read the words and their definitions. In your English notebook, write each word in a sentence that will help you remember the difference between the two words.

Word	Part of Speech	Definition
accept	verb	agree to, receive
except	preposition	not including, other than
affect	verb	to act on, to move (as in feelings)
effect	noun	the result or consequence of an action
allowed	verb	permitted
aloud	adverb	loudly, audibly
loose	adjective	not firmly or tightly fixed
lose	verb	cease to have
uninterested	adjective	not interested
disinterested	adjective	impartial, unbiased

woman	noun	one adult female
women	noun	more than one adult female

Colons and semicolons

Colon

A **colon** is two dots, one above the other. It looks like this.

:

A colon is used to mark off the main part of a sentence and introduce additional information such as a list. A colon can also be used to separate the speaker from their dialogue in a play script. Read the examples below.

colon Punctuation mark (:) that separates a general statement from one or more statements that give extra information, explanation or illustration. Statements after a colon do not have to be full sentences

» Just remember five things: thongs, towel, bathers, sunscreen and sunglasses.

» HAMLET: To be or not to be. That is the question.

12.9

Activity

1 Cross out the colons that are incorrect in the following sentences.

a The coach: told them what they needed to do: to win: play hard: keep their eyes on the ball: and to never give up.

b Don't bring nuts: on camp: Amanda and Ellie are allergic to them.

c She had two options left to her: eat the pie: or stay hungry.

d The trip was a failure: for two reasons: poor planning and terrible accommodation.

e Romeo: But soft: What light through yonder window breaks:

Semicolons

A **semicolon** consists of a dot above a comma. It looks like this.

;

semicolon Punctuation (;) used to join closely related clauses that could stand alone as sentences and can be used to separate long items in a list

A semicolon has two purposes:

» to show a relationship between two main clauses in a sentence (a main clause is one that could be used as a sentence in its own right)

» to separate items in a list when the individual items already have commas in them.

Read the examples below.

- I wanted to get a milkshake; she wanted a coke instead.
- The gift hamper was full of my favourite things: cashews, mint chocolate, dark chocolate; ripe, juicy strawberries; and two books from an author that I admired.

12.10

Activity

1 Punctuate the following short paragraphs correctly using semicolons, colons, commas and full stops in the spaces provided. You may also need to change some letters to capital letters.

a The holiday was great ☐ it was sunny ☐ it never rained ☐ we all got along and there was so much to do ☐ I wish Alex had been there ☐ he is always such fun ☐ the life of the party ☐

b I had forgotten how uncomfortable the house was ☐ water leaked through the roof ☐ floorboards creaked ☐ no door shut properly ☐ windows didn't close and there was a musty smell ☐ still we made our own fun ☐ it was the last time we were all together ☐

c I completely agree ☐ we have so many amazing animals and plants ☐ kangaroos ☐ wombats ☐ koalas and gum trees ☐

2 Cross out the incorrectly used punctuation in the following paragraph.

The dark clouds settled on the horizon; as the whales breached and blew water into the air. It was calving season and the mothers: and their babies were staying close together in the sheltered waters. We watched from the sand: me, Koro and Mum … or Mum's spirit, at least. I knew she was with us; she was always with us. When the rain started to fall we didn't move a muscle. We just pulled up the hoods of our jackets and huddled a little bit closer; this was family.

3 The following sentences are all punctuated incorrectly. Rewrite them with the correct punctuation.

a I slept through my alarm this morning, I had to run for the bus.

____

b Three people are staying at my house; my grandma, my grandpa and my aunt.

____

c My cat always sleeps in the warmest spot, today it's on top of my laptop.

____

Prepositions and prepositional phrases

A **preposition** is a word that indicates the position of one object in relation to something else. The word 'preposition' (pre + position) means 'to place before'. Prepositions usually come before a noun. The following is a table of common prepositions.

preposition A word class that usually describes the relationship between words in a sentence. Prepositions can indicate: space (e.g. 'on'), time (e.g. 'after') and other relationships (e.g. 'of', 'except')

Common prepositions				
aboard	about	across	after	against
along	amid	among	as	at
before	behind	below	beneath	beside
between	beyond	but	by	down
during	for	from	in	inside
into	near	of	off	on
onto	outside	over	past	round
through	to	towards	under	underneath
until	up	upon	with	within

12.11 Activity

1 Complete the following sentences by adding a suitable preposition in each space. There may be more than one correct answer.

a I can't wait ______________ the weekend.

b She parked ______________ the shopping centre.

c They queued for ages to get ______________ the venue.

d He climbed ______________ the tree to get a better view.

e They waded ______________ the mud to reach safety.

A **prepositional phrase** tells who is involved, or where, when or how something happens or takes place.

prepositional phrase A group of words that typically consists of a preposition followed by a noun group/phrase (e.g. 'on the train' in 'we met on the train'; 'on golf' in 'keen on golf')

For example:

» We had dinner at the restaurant. (where something takes places)

» She saw her yesterday afternoon. (when something takes place)

» I went to the show on the train. (how something takes place)

Activity

1 Highlight the prepositional phrase in each of the following sentences by focusing on where, when or how something takes place, indicated in the bracket.

a He jogged to the park near his house. (where?)

b I fell asleep during the movie. (when?)

c I ate lunch all by myself. (how?)

d I'm looking forward to going to the beach. (where?)

e I'll do my homework after dinner. (when?)

2 Add a prepositional phrase to the following clauses to make them more detailed and informative sentences.

a I found my overdue book ______________________________

b The train came ______________________________

c She rode her bike ______________________________

d He met his friends ______________________________

e They danced ______________________________

Register

'Register' is the level of formality in language. Writing well often relies on understanding what register is appropriate for your situation and **audience**. In spoken English and informal texts, we might end sentences with a preposition, but in very formal written English we should avoid doing this. For example, 'Where are you going to?' is fine in a novel or an informal letter or when talking to friends, but it should become 'Where are you going?' in a more formal situation.

audience An intended or assumed group of readers, listeners or viewers that a writer, designer, filmmaker or speaker is addressing

Activity

1 Rewrite the following sentences so that they have a formal register. You may need to do more than just remove the prepositions from the ends of sentences to do this.

a Hey, mate, where are you going to?

____

b That's the table you were supposed to put it on top of!

____

c That isn't the bowl of spag bol you were supposed to put the cheese onto.

____

Focus on spelling

Spelling used to be based on what words sounded like. This is called phonetic spelling. People in different regions may have spoken the same language but with different accents, so words were spelled differently from one region to the next. As more people learned to read and write, consistency in spelling became necessary simply so that people could understand each other. While English spelling conforms to some rules there are many exceptions and inconsistencies.

12.14

Activity

The table below shows some common spelling errors. Fill in the definitions, tips and an example sentence for each. Some have been completed for you.

Word	Definition/tips	Example sentence
advice		My teacher gave me some useful advice about spelling rules.
advise	'advise' is a verb; it means to give suggestions or recommendations	
a lot	'a lot' is always two words	
allot		
complement		Her bag complemented her shirt perfectly.
compliment	'compliment' meaning 'praise' is spelled with an 'i'	
lose		
loose	means 'not tight'; has two 'o's	
their	belonging to them	
there		
they're	short for 'they are'	

Proofreading, editing and redrafting

It is very important that you carefully proofread and **edit** your writing to correct any mistakes. Often, you will need to redraft and change some of your writing to improve it. Below is a list of helpful tips to ensure that your writing is as good as it can be.

Proofreading, editing and redrafting checklist		
To check	Action to take	Tick when complete
Is everything you have written relevant to the task or topic? Does any content need to be cut out?	Eliminate any content that does not serve the **purpose** of the piece of writing.	
Is your writing well organised? Does it follow a logical order, consistent with the type of text you are writing?	Sometimes a piece of evidence is better suited to a different paragraph, so move your points and evidence if necessary.	
Does your writing include enough detail and/or explanation?	If your ideas are not properly developed, add more information or explanation. An imaginative piece of writing may need more vivid description, and an informative piece may need more detail.	
Does your writing have a clear sense of purpose?	Add features that indicate the purpose of your writing. For example, if you are writing a persuasive piece, make sure you include persuasive devices and language.	
Are your sentences varied in length for interest and purpose?	Include a combination of simple, compound and complex sentences to keep your writing interesting and engaging.	
Are your sentences clearly expressed and grammatically correct?	Rewrite sentences that don't make sense or are overly long and unclear. Correct any mistakes you have made with noun–verb agreement and tenses.	
Is your spelling correct?	Fix any misspellings or autocorrected American spellings.	
Have you used punctuation accurately?	Make sure all sentences begin with a capital letter and end with the correct punctuation. All proper nouns should be capitalised. Apostrophes should only be used to indicate possession or contractions. Ensure commas are not used where a full stop should be or vice versa. Ensure dashes, brackets and other punctuation have been used correctly.	

edit To prepare, alter, adapt or refine with attention to grammar, spelling, punctuation and vocabulary
purpose An intended or assumed reason for a type of text

Glossary

adjective A word class that describes, identifies or quantifies a noun or a pronoun, e.g. two (number or quantity), my (possessive), ancient (descriptive), shorter (comparative), wooden (classifying).

adverb A word class that may modify a verb (e.g. 'softly' in 'the boy sings softly'), an adjective (e.g. 'really' in 'he is really strong') or another adverb (e.g. 'very' in 'the toddler walks very slowly').

aesthetic Concerned with a sense of beauty or an appreciation of artistic expression.

alliteration A recurrence of the same consonant sounds at the beginning of words in close succession (e.g. 'ripe, red raspberry').

assonance The repetition of vowel sounds within words (e.g. rain, main).

attitudes Particular ways of thinking and feeling towards people or things.

audience An intended or assumed group of readers, listeners or viewers that a writer, designer, filmmaker or speaker is addressing.

cinematography The science and art of shooting motion-picture scenes, including the camera work and lighting.

clause A grammatical unit referring to a happening or state e.g. 'the team won' (happening), 'the dog is red' (state), usually containing a subject and a verb group/phrase.

cohesion Grammatical or lexical relationships that bind different parts of a text together and give it unity. It is achieved through devices such as reference, substitution, repetition and text connectives.

colon Punctuation mark (:) that separates a general statement from one or more statements that give extra information, explanation or illustration. Statements after a colon do not have to be full sentences.

complex sentence A sentence with one or more subordinate clauses. In the following example, the subordinate clause is shown in brackets: I took my umbrella [because it was raining].

compound sentence A sentence with 2 or more main clauses of equal grammatical status, usually marked by a coordinating conjunction, e.g. [Ira came home this morning] [but he didn't stay long].

comprehension strategies Processes used by readers to make meaning from texts. They include activating and using prior knowledge, predicting likely future events in a text, monitoring meaning and critically reflecting.

conjunction In a sentence, a word that joins other words, groups/phrases or clauses together in a logical relationship such as addition, time, cause or comparison. There are 2 types: coordinating and subordinating.

connective Words linking, and logically relating ideas to one another, in paragraphs and sentences indicating relationships of time, cause and effect, comparison, addition, condition and concession or clarification.

context An environment or situation (social, cultural or historical) in which a text is responded to or created. Or wording surrounding an unfamiliar word, which a reader or listener uses to understand its meaning.

contraction An abbreviated version of a word or words, often formed by shortening a word or merging 2 words into one (e.g. doctor: Dr; do not: don't).

convention An accepted practice that has developed over time and is generally used and understood (e.g. use of punctuation).

dialect Form of a language distinguished by features of vocabulary, grammar and pronunciation particular to a region.

edit To prepare, alter, adapt or refine with attention to grammar, spelling, punctuation and vocabulary.

hybrid text A composite text resulting from a purposeful mixing of elements from different sources or genres (e.g. 'infotainment').

idiom An expression whose meaning does not relate to the literal meaning of its words (e.g. 'They went out to paint the town red').

imagery Visually descriptive or figurative language to represent things including objects, actions and ideas in ways that appeal to the senses of the reader or viewer.

imperative verb A verb that gives an order or instruction (e.g. 'open the door').

jargon Technical words specific to a certain group, such as medical or legal jargon.

language features Features that support meaning e.g. clause- and word-level grammar, vocabulary, figurative language, punctuation, images. Choices vary for the purpose, subject matter, audience and mode or medium.

literary text Past and contemporary texts across a range of cultural contexts which are valued for their form and style and are recognised as having artistic value.

metalanguage Vocabulary including technical terms, concepts, ideas or codes used to describe or discuss a language. The language of grammar and the language of literary criticism are examples.

metaphor A type of figurative language used to describe a person or object through an implicit comparison to something with similar characteristics.

mise en scène In film, the composition of a shot, including elements such as lighting, costumes, props, set design and special effects.

modal verb A verb that expresses a degree of probability attached by a speaker or writer to a statement (e.g. 'I might come home') or a degree of obligation (e.g. 'You must give it to me').

mode Various processes of communication – listening, speaking, reading or viewing and writing or creating.

multimodal A combination of 2 or more communication modes (e.g. print, image and spoken text, as in film or computer presentations).

narrative The selection and sequencing of events or experiences, real or imagined, to tell a story to entertain, engage, inform and extend imagination, typically using an orientation, complication and resolution.

noun A word class that includes all words denoting person, place, object or thing, idea or emotion. Nouns may be common, proper, collective, abstract and compound.

perspective A lens through which the author perceives the world and creates a text, or the lens through which the reader or viewer perceives the world and understands a text.

phrase A group of words often beginning with a preposition but without a subject and verb combination (e.g. 'on the river'; 'with brown eyes').

point of view The position from which the text is designed to be perceived (e.g. a narrator might take a role of first or third person, omniscient or restricted in knowledge of events or the opinion presented in a text)

prefix A meaningful element (morphemes) added to the beginning of a word to change its meaning (e.g. 'un' to 'happy' to make 'unhappy').

preposition A word class that usually describes the relationship between words in a sentence. Prepositions can indicate space (e.g. 'on'), time (e.g. 'after') and other relationships (e.g. 'of', 'except').

prepositional phrase A group of words that typically consists of a preposition followed by a noun group/phrase (e.g. 'on the train' in 'we met on the train'; 'on golf' in 'keen on golf').

pronoun A word that takes the place of a noun (e.g. I, me, he, she, herself, you, it, that, they, few, many, who, whoever, someone, everybody, and many others).

protagonist The main character in a text.

purpose An intended or assumed reason for a type of text.

salience A strategy of emphasis, highlighting what is important in a text. In images, it is achieved through strategies such as the placement of an item in the foreground, size and contrast in tone or colour.

scan To read, moving one's eyes quickly down a page seeking specific words and phrases. It is also used when a reader first finds information to determine whether it will answer their questions.

semicolon Punctuation (;) used to join closely related clauses that could stand alone as sentences and can be used to separate long items in a list.

simile A device comparing 2 things that are not alike. Similes use 'like', 'as' or 'than' to make the comparison (e.g. The cake was as light as air).

skim Reading quickly, selecting key words and details through a text to determine the general meaning or main messages or ideas.

Standard Australian English Recognised as the 'common language' of Australians, it is the dynamic and evolving spoken and written English used for official or public purposes, and recorded in dictionaries, style guides and grammars.

style The distinctive language features, text structures and/or subject matter in a text which may shape meaning, be enjoyed for its aesthetic qualities or distinguish the work of an author, period etc.

subject A word or group of words (usually a noun group/phrase) in a sentence or clause representing the person, thing or idea doing the action that follows (e.g. 'The dog [subject] was barking').

subject matter The topic or theme under consideration.

subordinating conjunction Words that introduce clauses that add or extend information. They include conjunctions such as 'after', 'when', 'because', 'if' and 'that'.

suffix An element added to the end of a word to change its meaning (e.g. to form past tense: '-ed'; to show a smaller amount or degree: -less; to form an adverb: -ly).

symbolism The use of one object, person or situation to signify or represent another by giving them meanings that are different from their literal sense (e.g. a dove is a symbol of peace).

synonym A word having nearly the same meaning as others (e.g. synonyms for 'old' include 'aged', 'venerable', 'antiquated').

tense The form a verb takes to signal the location of a clause in time (e.g. present tense 'has' in 'Jo has a cat' locates the situation in the present; past tense 'had' in 'Jo had a cat' locates it in the past).

theme The main idea, concept or message of a text.

tone The mood created by the language features used by an author and the way the text makes the reader feel.

values Ideas and beliefs specific to individuals and groups.

verb A word class that expresses processes that include doing, feeling, thinking, saying and relating.

verb group Consists of a main verb, alone or preceded by one or more auxiliary or modal verbs as modifiers.

visual features Visual components of a text which may include placement, salience, framing, representation of action or reaction, shot size, social distance and camera angle.

voice The distinct personality of a piece of writing; the individual writing style of the composer, created through the way they use and mix various language features (e.g. a narrative using a child's voice).

Acknowledgements

Insight Publications thanks the following writers for their contributions to *Australian Curriculum* English Year 8: Leanne Bondin and Adam Kealley.

Insight Publications is also grateful to the following individuals and organisations for permission to reproduce copyright material.

Texts: Extract: *Parvana* by Deborah Ellis, Allen & Unwin, (Crows Nest NSW, 2002); Extract: *The Hobbit* by JRR Tolkien, HarperCollins UK; Extract: *The Bad Beginning (A Series of Unfortunate Events)* by Lemony Snicket, Egmont.; Extract: UN speech by Malala Yousafzai, malala.org; Extract: 'My Country' by Dorothea Mackellar, Curtis Brown Australia; 'My Country by' Oscar Krahnvohl; Extract: 'My Story' by Alicia Bates, in *Growing up Aboriginal in Australia*, Black Inc.; Extract: Anne Frank: *The Diary of a Young Girl*, Penguin Books UK; Blog post: Syria: I am Aleppo, Aleppo is Me, by Marcell Shehwaro, https://globalvoices.org/2014/03/12/syria-i-am-aleppo-aleppo-is-me/ ; Extract: *Hive* by A.J. Betts, Pan Macmillan Australia; Extract: *Rogue* by A.J. Betts, Pan Macmillan Australia; Poem: 'Wake Up' by Jesse Oliver; Poem: 'The the Impotence of Proofreading' by Taylor Mali; Play extract: 'Scrambled Eggs' by Sue Murray; Extract: *Don't Call Me Ishmael* by Michael Gerard Bauer, First published by Omnibus Books, an imprint of Scholastic Australia Pty Ltd, 2006, Text copyright © Michael Gerard Bauer, 2006, Cover and text illustrations copyright © Michael Gerard Bauer, 2006, Reproduced with permission from Scholastic Australia Pty Limited.; Extract: *Young Dark Emu: A Truer History* by Bruce Pascoe, Magabala Books (Broome, 2019); Speech: We Shall Fight on the Beaches, by Winston Churchill, Reproduced with permission of Curtis Brown, London on behalf of The Estate of Winston S. Churchill, The Estate of Winston S. Churchill; Blog Post: 'Dog Descended from Wild Animals', *The Shovel,* Extract: THE HUNGER GAMES by Suzanne Collins, Copyright © 2008 by Suzanne Collins, Reprinted by permission of Scholastic Inc.; Extract: *Bridie's Fire* by Kirsty Murray, Allen & Unwin, (Crows Nest NSW, 2003); Extract: *Bindi*, 'Being Bindi' by Kirli Saunders, Magabala Books (Broome, 2020); Extract: *Revolution is not a Dinner Party*, by Ying Chan Compestine, Penguin Books UK; Extract: Interview of Seaman Dan by Henry Gibson Dan; Web Extract: What is animal experimentation Centre of the Cell is a science education centre based at Queen Mary, University of London, https://www.centreofthecell.org/animal-experimentation/what-is-animal-experimentation/; Poem extract: 'Totally like whatever, you know?'©2023 Taylor Mali.

Images: Cover Image: *Soul Surfer: A True Story of Faith, Family, and Fighting to Get Back on the Board*, Simon & Schuster, MTV Books (June 6, 2006); Adopt, DON'T BUY - PETA; Cover Image: *True Spirit: The Aussie girl who took on the world*, Simon & Schuster, Pedigree advertisement; CINDERELLA, Cinderella, 1950, ©Walt Disney Pictures/courtesy Everett Collection; Modern Cinderella, Elizabeth Howlett; Goldilocks, Elizabeth Howlett; Goldilocks Rocks, Capstone Publishing; Copyright retained by Movember, 2012 campaign; Cover Image: *Hive* by A.J. Betts (2018), Pan Macmillan; Cover Image: *Rogue: The Vault Book 2* by A.J. Betts (2019), Pan Macmillan; Jesse Oliver; Screenshot: Australia SOTE 2021, https://soe.dcceew.gov.au/indigenous/introduction; Infographic: Seasonal fire management; credit to Indigenous Desert Alliance and the 10 Deserts; Infographic: Richmond Valley Fire management in National Parks, © State of New South Wales (Department of Planning and Environment) [2023] RED DOG: TRUE BLUE photography by David Darcy, courtesy of Good Dog Enterprises. The following images from Alamy: Covid, Fire stick farming, Lego, *Percy Jackson & the Olympians film poster*, Propaganda poster. Additional images from Pexels, Shutterstock Unsplash and Wikimedia Commons.